THE BEST OF The MAILBOX Magazine

The Best of The MAILBOX

Preschool—Book 2

Departments

3	Crafts for Little Hands
15	Songs & Such
23	Fingerplays, Poems, & Rhymes
31	It's Circle Time
39	Get Moving!
45	Busy Hands
51	Learning Centers
63	Getting Your Ducklings in a Row
69	Bulletin Boards and Displays
83	Our Readers Write

Theme Units

90	Preschoolers, Start Your Engines!
98	Fishing for Names
104	Pumpkin Science
110	My Family and Me!
114	Weather Wise
120	'Twas the Night Before…
128	To Market, to Market
133	Get Heart Happy!
140	Every Chick Counts
144	Beautiful Butterflies
150	A "14-Carrot" Collection
154	Red, White, and Blue Gala
160	Backyard Barbecue
166	Slides, Swings, and Playground Things!
172	See You Later, Alligator!

Special Features

178	Get Spotted at the Library!
181	Welcome to Open House!
184	Golden Opportunities
186	Snap! Button! Z-z-z-i-p!
188	If You're Happy and You Know It
191	Classroom by Design

About This Book

Packed with loads of our most popular ideas, *The Best of* **The Mailbox**® *Preschool—Book 2* is the perfect resource for energizing your early childhood classroom! The editors of *The Mailbox*® have compiled the best teacher-tested ideas published in the 1999–2003 issues of the preschool magazine to bring you this valuable and timesaving resource. Inside you'll find hundreds of fun and practical ideas featured in our regular departments, including arts and crafts; learning centers; circle time; and songs, poems, and fingerplays; as well as special thematic units. *The Best of* **The Mailbox**® *Preschool—Book 2* is *the* best resource for a classroom filled with fun and learning!

Managing Editor: Susan Walker
Editor at Large: Diane Badden
Staff Editor: Leanne Stratton
Copy Editors: Tazmen Carlisle, Amy Kirtley-Hill, Karen L. Mayworth, Kristy Parton, Debbie Shoffner, Cathy Edwards Simrell
Art Coordinators: Theresa Lewis Goode, Stuart Smith
Artists: Pam Crane, Theresa Lewis Goode, Clevell Harris, Ivy L. Koonce, Clint Moore, Greg D. Rieves, Rebecca Saunders, Barry Slate, Stuart Smith, Donna K. Teal
The Mailbox® **Books.com:** Judy P. Wyndham (MANAGER); Jennifer Tipton Bennett (DESIGNER/ARTIST); Karen White (INTERNET COORDINATOR); Paul Fleetwood, Xiaoyun Wu (SYSTEMS)

President, The Mailbox Book Company™**:** Joseph C. Bucci
Director of Book Planning and Development: Chris Poindexter
Curriculum Director: Karen P. Shelton
Book Development Managers: Cayce Guiliano, Elizabeth H. Lindsay, Thad McLaurin
Editorial Planning: Kimberley Bruck (MANAGER); Debra Liverman, Sharon Murphy, Susan Walker (TEAM LEADERS)
Editorial and Freelance Management: Karen A. Brudnak; Sarah Hamblet, Hope Rodgers (EDITORIAL ASSISTANTS)
Editorial Production: Lisa K. Pitts (TRAFFIC MANAGER); Lynette Dickerson (TYPE SYSTEMS); Mark Rainey (TYPESETTER)
Librarian: Dorothy C. McKinney

www.themailbox.com

Manufactured in the United States
10 9 8 7 6 5 4 3 2

Crafts for Little Hands

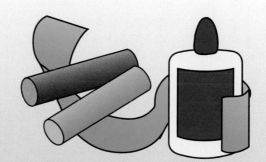

Crafts for Little Hands

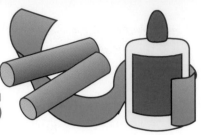

Handprint Crabs

Teach youngsters to crab-walk (walk on hands and feet with tummy facing up); then invite them to crab-walk right over to your art center to make these snappy crabs! To make one, a child dips her hands into washable red tempera paint. Then she presses them onto a sheet of construction paper so that the palm prints overlap and the fingerprints extend in opposite directions. When the paint is dry, she draws on a smile, then draws an eye on each thumbprint. Finally, she glues sand underneath the crab to complete the picture. These cute crustaceans can't be beat!

Kimberly Calhoun—PreK
Tutor Time Learning Center
Apex, NC

"A-peel-ing" Apples

For a colorful display, try these translucent apples. To make one apple, draw a simple apple and stem outline on a piece of white paper. Tape a piece of clear plastic wrap or a resealable plastic bag over the drawing. Squeeze white glue along the outline; then press yarn onto it, making sure to include the stem to create a loop. Allow the glue to dry. Next, tint glue with red, yellow, or green food coloring. Use a paintbrush to paint a thick coat of the glue on the plastic, inside the dried yarn. Let the glue dry for a day. Peel the apple decoration from the plastic; then suspend it. Apples, apples everywhere!

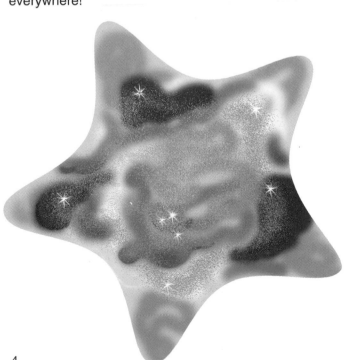

"Sense-ational" Starfish

This craft uses a fabulous textured paint with lots of sensory appeal! To prepare, mix several different colors of puff paint. For each color, combine two tablespoons of washable tempera paint and one-third cup of white glue. Fold in two cups of non-mentholated shaving cream until the color is well blended. (For best results, use the paint soon after mixing it.)

To make one starfish, fingerpaint a star-shaped tagboard cutout with several colors of the puff paint. Sprinkle glitter over the wet paint; then set the starfish aside to dry overnight. Youngsters will enjoy smelling, touching, and seeing this interesting paint—even when it's dry!

Beverly Folena—PreK
Creative Kids Preschool
Placerville, CA

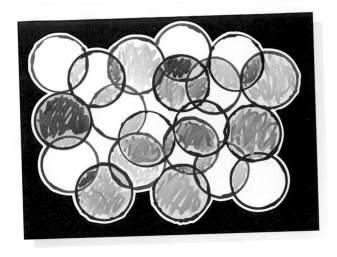

Paper Cup Printing

Focus on circles with this well-rounded painting project! First, set out a few different colors of tempera paint in shallow containers. Provide a supply of paper drinking cups and white construction paper. Have each youngster dip the rim of a paper cup into the paint color of her choice and then print it onto her paper. Have her continue with other colors, overlapping the circles as she desires. When the paint is dry, invite her to use crayons or markers to color in the areas created by the overlapping circles. Then help her cut around the perimeter of her design and glue it onto a sheet of black construction paper for a dazzling work of art!

Carrie Lacher
Friday Harbor, WA

Proud As Peacocks

Are your children as proud as peacocks to be preschoolers? Have them make these colorful peacocks for display. To make one, round the corners of eight paint samples. Holding all eight samples in hand, arrange them to create a fan; then staple them together. Cut a peacock shape (pattern on page 14) from blue construction paper; then glue the shape onto the fan of samples. Use a marker to add an eye on each peacock along with a personalized message. Display the projects together with students' photographs in a visible area of your school.

Barb Stefaniuk—Preschool
Kerrobert Tiny Tots Playschool
Kerrobert, Saskatchewan, Canada

Lei is a proud preschooler!

Bloomin' Apple Trees

Real apple trees bloom in the spring and ripen in the fall. This apple tree craft blooms and ripens right before your eyes! Provide each child with a construction paper apple tree. Then invite her to use a red bingo marker to dab circles on the treetop. When the ink is dry, have the child use a brown crayon or marker to add apple stems. Next, have the child turn over her tree and glue on crumpled pink and white tissue paper squares to represent blossoms. Hang each child's tree in your room and you'll have a crafty orchard of blooming apple trees!

Puzzle-Piece Tree

If you have a jigsaw puzzle with missing pieces, this is the project for you! Have each child draw a tree trunk and branches on a sheet of construction paper. (Draw the trees in advance for younger children.) Provide pieces from an old jigsaw puzzle, the kind with a few hundred pieces. Have each youngster glue puzzle pieces to the branches of her tree to resemble the colorful leaves of autumn. Encourage each child to add a few "leaves" falling from the tree or lying on the ground to complete the seasonal effect.

Doris Porter—Preschool
Aquin System Preschool
Cascade, IA

Mummy Madness

Your little ones will go mad for these marvelous mummies! To make one, trace a person shape onto sturdy white paper (a large gingerbread-man cookie cutter works well as a tracer). Cut out the shape. Using a glue mat to protect the tabletop, spread white glue that has been thinned with a small amount of water onto the cutout. Cover the glue with torn strips of white tissue paper or toilet tissue to resemble a mummy's wrappings. Cut two black eyes from construction paper; then glue them on the mummy's face. Mount the completed project on an orange background. Looks like Halloween decorating is all wrapped up!

Christa J. Koch—PreK
Circle of Friends
Bethlehem, PA

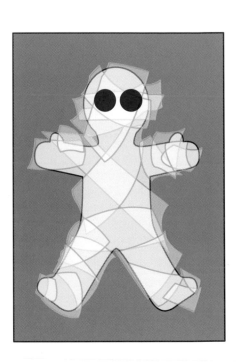

Ticklish Bats

These bats look "vonderful" on bulletin board paper murals or T-shirts. To create a bat, paint the bottom of a child's foot. Use black fabric paint if the print will go on a shirt or washable black tempera paint if the print will go on a mural. Have the child press his footprint onto the fabric or paper; then wipe his foot clean. Paint the child's other foot. Help the child press this print so that the heels overlap as shown. Wipe the foot clean. Use a small paintbrush to add ears. When the paint is dry, use fabric paint (on the shirt) or regular paint to add eyes.

Jan Wicker—Four-Year-Olds
First Presbyterian Preschool
Roanoke Rapids, NC

Dynamite Dinos

These paper-plate projects make for prehistoric preschool fun! In advance, use a black marker to draw the body parts of a dinosaur on a thin white paper plate as shown. To make a dinosaur, cut out the pieces. Help the child attach the head, arm, and leg to the dinosaur body with metal brads. Then have her use crayons or markers to decorate the dino as desired. Will your dinosaur be fierce or friendly?

Lisa Scaglione—Four- and Five-Year-Olds
Children's Village Preschool
Sherrill's Ford, NC

Pumpkins on the Vine

This "hand-some" painting project features a mighty fine vine! For each child, use a green marker to draw a curvy line across a sheet of white construction paper. Have a child make a fist and then dip her fingers into a shallow bowl of orange tempera paint as shown. Next, help her press the painted part of her fist onto the green line to make a pumpkin shape. Have her repeat this process to make a few more pumpkins along the vine. Then encourage her to finish the picture by using green paint to make thumbprints for pumpkin stems and leaves.

Sarah Booth—Four- and Five-Year-Olds
Messiah Nursery School, South Williamsport, PA

Flying Turkeys!

To make a hanging turkey project, tie a knot at one end of a length of yarn. Poke a hole in the center of the side of a large foam cup; then, starting inside the cup, pull the yarn through the hole. Poke colorful craft feathers into the cup as shown. Finish the turkey by gluing paper eyes and a paper beak to the end of the cup. Hang these turkeys where they are safe from the cook!

Helen K. Dening, Silver Creek, NY

Welcome!

Need a great gift idea for parents? Have each child make a wintry welcome mat with his own two feet! In advance, visit a local carpet store and request donations of dark-colored carpet samples. To make a welcome mat, paint a child's feet with white fabric paint; then have him make footprints on a carpet sample. Next, use Slick fabric paint to print a greeting and the child's name on the carpet. When the paint is dry, have the child use fabric paint to decorate the footprints to resemble snowmen. This gift is sure to melt the heart of the lucky recipient!

Jami Haarz—Preschool
Scribbles School, Lapeer, MI

Crafty Candy Canes

This holiday craft not only looks great, but also provides youngsters with plenty of patterning practice. In advance, collect two paper towel tubes for each child in your class. Have the child paint one tube red and one tube white. When the tubes are dry, help him cut each one into six pieces. Next, provide the child with a 24-inch length of floral wire; then have him thread the tube pieces onto the wire, alternating the colors. Bend the ends of the wire around the edges of the top and bottom pieces; then have the child bend the wire into the shape of a candy cane. To display these sweet crafts, tie a length of yarn around the curve of each cane; then hang the canes around your classroom.

Ann Rand—Three-Year-Olds
The Principia Preschool, St. Louis, MO

Decaf Santa

Ho! Ho! Ho! To make one of these Santas, cut a six-inch triangle from red construction paper. Glue the triangle to a flattened coffee filter as shown. Glue cotton balls onto the top and bottom of the hat. Use markers to add facial features to the filter; then trim around the edges to create Santa's beard. Jolly good work!

Shelly Wooldridge—Preschool, Smithville Elementary School
Smithville, WV

Dandy Candy

'Tis the season for these pretty peppermints! To make one, have a child paint red and green alternating stripes on the rim of a small white paper plate. After the paint dries, help the child wrap the plate in a piece of clear plastic wrap or cellophane. Then twist the ends of the wrap and tie a length of red curling ribbon around each one.

Michelle LeMaster-Johnson—Four-Year-Olds
Windlake Elementary
Milwaukee, WI

Winter Snow Scene

Use spools as tools to make this wintry picture! Glue brown paper tree trunks with green paper trees to a sheet of blue construction paper. Then dip one end of an empty thread spool into white tempera paint and press it onto the scene to make a snowflake. Use spools in various sizes to add as much snow as you like. Brrr!

Debbie Ellingworth, Wadena, MN

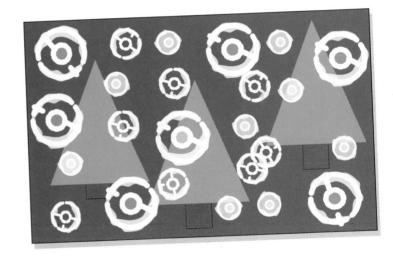

Smashing Snowman

From potatoes to painting, there's one kitchen tool that can do it all. So bring a potato masher to your classroom to make these cool snowmen! Have a child dip the masher into white tempera paint and then press it onto blue construction paper three times to make the three parts of a snowman's body. Allow the paint to dry overnight. The next day, help the child glue on precut felt features, such as a carrot nose and a hat. Add sticky dots to the snowman and use a marker to give it two twig arms. These snowmen are simply smashing!

Kandi Webster
Hattiesburg, MS

Celery Roses

Sure, celery is good for a healthy snack, but is it good for *painting?* Of course! A bunch of celery makes these realistic roses—perfect for a Valentine's Day greeting! To prepare, cut off the bottom two inches from a bunch of celery (leave the rubber band in place to hold together any stalks that come loose). Next, dry the bunch with a paper towel, or allow it to air-dry. Have a child dip the bottom of the bunch into red paint and then print a few roses near the top of a sheet of white construction paper. Have her add green fingerpainted stems and glue on a flowerpot cutout. Then write a Valentine's Day message at the top and the child's name on the pot.

Molly Mosely—PreK
Wee Little Ones Preschool
Pana, IL

Shamrock Showcase

Need a unique art technique? You're in luck with this shamrock collage. In advance, visit a local fabric store and purchase a variety of green fabric remnants. Then use pinking shears to cut the remnants into small squares. To make a collage, dip the squares into a mixture that is half water and half glue; then arrange the scraps on a sheet of white construction paper so that they overlap. When the glue is dry, use a permanent marker to draw a shamrock outline on the fabric. Then cut out the shamrock and glue it to a green sheet of construction paper. If desired, arrange the shamrocks together on a wall for a great green display!

Michele Menzel
Appleton, WI

Valentine Boxes

These boxes are red, white, and just right for taking home valentines! To make one, first spray-paint a class supply of empty tissue boxes red. Then set out heart-shaped sponges and white tempera paint in shallow containers. Have a child sponge-paint hearts all over a red tissue box. When the paint is dry, use a permanent marker to label the box with the child's name. On the day of your party, slip valentines into the box openings and youngsters will have sturdy totes to carry home their cards!

Sarah Booth—Four- and Five-Year-Olds
Messiah Nursery School
South Williamsport, PA

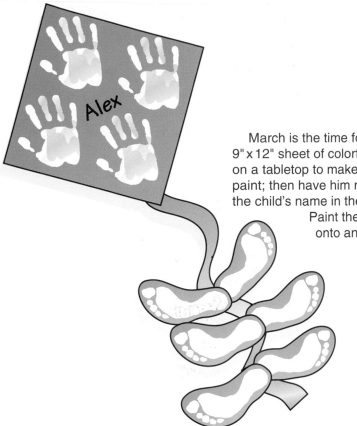

Welcome, Wind!

March is the time for kite making, and these personalized kites are cool! Cut a 9" x 12" sheet of colorful construction paper into a nine-inch square. Turn the square on a tabletop to make a diamond shape. Paint a child's hand with white tempera paint; then have him make handprints on the paper as shown. Use a marker to print the child's name in the center. Next, have the child remove his shoes and socks. Paint the bottoms of his bare feet with white paint; then have him step onto another different-colored sheet of construction paper. Repeat this step twice to make a total of six footprints. When the paint is dry, cut around the footprints. Tape one end of a length of ribbon or crepe paper streamer to the back of the diamond; then tape the footprint cutouts to the ribbon to resemble bows. Now go fly a kite!

Donna Price—Infant–Preschool
Creative Kids Learning Center
Salt Lake City, UT

Rainbow Bracelets

These beautiful bracelets sport the colors of the rainbow! For each child, cut six one-inch-wide loops from paper towel or toilet paper tubes. Have each youngster paint one loop in each of the colors of the rainbow—red, orange, yellow, green, blue, and purple. When the paint is completely dry, ask the child to string the loops (in any order she wishes) onto a pipe cleaner. Wrap the pipe cleaner around her wrist and twist the ends together to secure the bracelet. What a colorful accessory!

Betty Silkunas
Lower Gwynedd Elementary
Ambler, PA

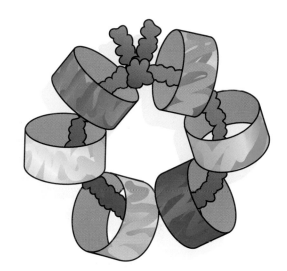

...Out Like a Lamb!

Herald in spring with these magnetic little lambs! To make one lamb, cut a three-inch circle from heavy white poster board and a 1½-inch circle from black craft foam. Have a child glue the circles together as shown. Next, have her glue cotton balls onto the larger circle and then glue a piece of a cotton ball to the head. Have the child glue on paper eyes, black felt ears, and black felt feet. Place a self-adhesive magnet strip to the back of the lamb and your little sheep's complete!

Lovely Swans

Swim into spring with these simple swans! To make one, cut a thin white paper plate in half; then cut away the rim of the plate from one half. Glue the rim to the intact plate half, as shown, to form the swan's neck. Then glue on an orange construction paper beak and add a sticky dot eye. Add a few pretty white craft feathers to complete this beautiful bird!

Leita Oberhofer, Newport News, VA

Excellent Eggs

The Easter bunny never had eggs like these! To prepare, purchase a class supply of foam eggs (available at craft stores). Cut colorful wrapping paper into one-inch squares. Provide each child with an egg, a small paintbrush, and a cup of glue. Have her use the brush to cover the egg with glue. Then have her press wrapping paper squares onto the egg. Encourage the child to overlap the squares, cover the entire egg with paper, and then brush a thin layer of glue over the egg. Set the egg on a sheet of waxed paper to dry. To create an eye-catching display, fill a basket with Easter grass and arrange the eggs in it. Excellent!

Debby Moon—Preschool
School for Little People
Wichita Falls, TX

Mother's Day Magnet

These flower magnets make attractive gifts for Mother's Day! In advance, color some rotini pasta in a variety of floral colors. Break each colored pasta piece in half. For each child, cut a two-inch circle from white poster board or tagboard. Use a pencil to draw a small center circle. To assemble a magnet, cover the small inner circle with tacky glue; then sprinkle on some millet birdseed. Allow the glue to dry. Then spread tacky glue over the remainder of the cutout circle and arrange the pasta "petals" around the millet center. Glue on a tagboard stem and leaves; then add a length of self-adhesive magnetic tape to the back of the flower. Have each youngster take her magnet home, along with a Mother's Day message, to post on the fridge!

adapted from an idea by Jane Walker—PreK
Hubbard Pre-K
Forsyth, GA

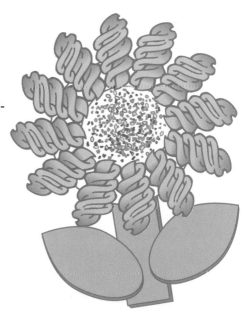

Open Wide!

Folks are sure to say, "Aaah" when they see these awesome alligators! To make one alligator, tear green paper to make the alligator's long body. Next, tear another long piece for the tail and then glue it to the body. Continue tearing pieces and gluing them together until the alligator has jaws and legs. Add torn white and black paper eyes. And, of course, don't forget to give the alligator lots of sharp, white teeth! Display the alligators on a swamp scene made with blue plastic wrap and torn-paper trees and plants. Onlookers will be awed by the different sizes and shapes of alligators! Awesome!

Julie Shields—PreK
Brookeland School
Brookeland, TX

Paper Plate Crabs

In a pinch? This craft's a cinch! To make one, paint the back of a paper plate orange. When the paint is dry, fold the plate in half and staple the edges together. Glue on a pair of black pom-pom eyes and construction paper claws and legs. Quick and cute!

Nicole Petro—Preschool
Wee Vikes Learning Center
Glen Gardner, NJ

Fabulous Fireworks

Your youngsters will get a bang out of this unique painting project! Provide a child with a large sheet of white paper. Next, have her squirt a small drop of liquid tempera paint onto the paper and then cover the paint with a margarine-tub lid. Have the child disperse the paint by hitting the center of the lid with a wooden mallet or block. To create more colorful fireworks, invite the child to squirt a different color of paint over the first color and repeat the procedure. Help the child sprinkle glitter over her completed fireworks and then set the painting aside to dry.

Marsha Feffer—PreK
Bentley Early Childhood Center
Salem, MA

Pattern
Use with "Proud As Peacocks" on page 5.

SONGS & SUCH

Here We Go Round the Birthday Cake

This personalized birthday song will have your little ones huffing, puffing, and giggling! During a group time, lead children in circling around the birthday boy or girl as they sing the first verse of the following song. Then have them circle around in the opposite direction as they sing the second verse. Invite the honoree to pretend to blow out the candles (her classmates). Your preschoolers will giggle with delight as they fall to the floor!

(sung to the tune of "The Mulberry Bush")

Here we go round the birthday cake, the birthday cake, the birthday cake.
Here we go round the birthday cake.
Today is [child's name]'s birthday!

Make a wish and blow us out, blow us out, blow us out.
Make a wish and blow us out.
Today is [child's name]'s birthday!

Karen Eiben and Melinda Wilson—Preschool
The Kids' Place Child Development Center, LaSalle, IL

Wash Your Hands

Invite youngsters to join you in clapping and singing while they wait in line to wash their hands. You might want to post a copy of the song near your sink as a reminder. You'll sing those germs away!

(sung to the tune of "Yankee Doodle")

Wash your hands before you eat.
Wash those germs away.
Use soap and water; rinse them off.
You'll have clean hands today!

Soap your hands and rub, rub, rub!
Wash those germs away.
Rinse with water; pat them dry.
You'll have clean hands today!

Suzanne Moore

I'm a Firefighter

(sung to the tune of "I'm a Little Teapot")

I'm a firefighter.   *Point to self.*
Here's my hose.   *Outstretch arm with finger pointed.*
I put out fires,
As everyone knows.
When I see a fire,   *Hand over brow.*
I douse it out.   *Outstretch arm with finger pointed.*
"Thank you! Thank you!"
People shout.

Linda Rice Ludlow
Bethesda Christian School
Brownsburg, IN

I'm a Little Scarecrow

(sung to the tune of "I'm a Little Teapot")

I'm a little scarecrow
Stuffed with hay.
Here I stand in a field all day.
When I see the crows,
I like to shout,
"Hey! You crows, you better get out!"

Abby Carney—Three-Year-Olds
Kid's Connection
S. Hamilton, MA

Kelly Williams, Jacksboro, TX

Did You Ever See a Turkey?

Reinforce color recognition with this turkey tune. In advance, cut out a class supply of red, brown, yellow, and orange construction paper feathers. Give each child one feather. As the class sings the song below, have each student hold up his feather when its color is mentioned.

(sung to the tune of "Did You Ever See a Lassie?")

Did you ever see a turkey, a turkey, a turkey
As he struts around the farmyard with feathers so bright?
With red ones and brown ones and yellow ones and orange ones,
Did you ever see a turkey with feathers so bright?

Cele McCloskey and Brenda Peters, Dallastown, PA

Kwanzaa Candles

(sung to the tune of "Ten Little Indians")

One little, two little, three little candles,
Four little, five little, six little candles,
Seven little candles shine for Kwanzaa,
Shining and glowing in the night!

Red little, green little, black little candles,
Nice little, bright little Kwanzaa candles.
Shine, little candles, shine for Kwanzaa.
Oh, what a beautiful sight!

Lucia Kemp Henry

Santa Had a Christmas Tree

Add to the fun of this tune by preparing a few props. Gather the following items: a paper star covered with glitter, a jingle bell, a paper Christmas bulb and a box wrapped in holiday paper. (Put a couple of marbles or blocks in the box so it will rattle when shaken.) Ask four student volunteers to hold the items in front of the group as you sing. As each item is mentioned in the song, have the designated child hold it up or shake it to make a noise.

(sung to the tune of "Old MacDonald Had a Farm")

Santa had a Christmas tree,
Ho, ho, ho, ho, ho!
And on that tree he had a star,
Ho, ho, ho, ho, ho!
With a twinkle, twinkle here
And a twinkle, twinkle there,
Here a twinkle, there a twinkle,
Everywhere a twinkle, twinkle!
Santa had a Christmas tree,
Ho, ho, ho, ho, ho!

Continue with additional verses:

And on that tree he had a bell…With a jingle, jingle here…
And on that tree he had a light…With a sparkle, sparkle here…
And under that tree he had a gift…With a rattle, rattle here…

Diana Shepard—Toddlers, First Presbyterian Preschool, Wilmington, NC

I'm a Little Snowman

(sung to the tune of "I'm a Little Teapot")

I'm a little snowman, short and stout,
Sticks for arms and a carrot snout.
When the weather warms up, gosh, oh, gee!
I melt and there's no more of me!

Jan Payne—Preschool
Dodge County Even Start Program
Eastman, GA

Happy New Year!

Get ready to ring in a new year with this lively tune. Are you ready? 10…9…8…

(sung to the tune of "Head, Shoulders, Knees, and Toes")

There's a new year on the way,
On the way!
There's a new year on the way,
On the way!
Let's celebrate the year and give a cheer!   *Say, "Hooray!"*
There's a new year on the way,
On the way!

It's Freezing, It's Snowing

What happens after a long, cold night of snow? You wake up to a world all aglow!

(sung to the tune of "A Tisket, a Tasket")

It's freezing. It's snowing.
The old wind is blowing.
I went to bed, laid down my head,
All the time not knowing,
Not knowing, not knowing,
The wind and snow kept going.
I woke up from a dark cold night
To see the world aglowing!

Rebecca Fisch—PreK, Yeshiva Rabbi Hirsch, Brooklyn, NY

Will You Be Mine?

This colorful song and activity reinforces color recognition! To prepare, cut out a class supply of red, pink, and white construction paper hearts. Next, make a miniature mailbox by covering a shoebox with colored Con-Tact paper and then cutting a slot in the lid. To begin the activity, provide each child with a construction paper heart. Then direct each student to place his valentine in the box when the color is mentioned in the song.

(sung to the tune of "Mary Had a Little Lamb")

Mail your [red] heart valentines,
Valentines, valentines!
Mail your [red] heart valentines,
And send love, oh so fine!

Repeat, replacing the underlined word with pink *and* white *in turn.*

I mailed my friend a valentine,
Valentine, valentine!
I mailed my friend a valentine,
And sent my love so fine!

LeeAnn Collins
Mason, MI

I'm a Little Bunny

Easter brings about bunches of bunnies. So teach youngsters the following tune and invite them to get hopping!

(sung to the tune of "I'm a Little Teapot")

I'm a little bunny.
See me hop.
Watch my ears go flippity-flop.
My tail is soft as cotton. Look and see!
My nose wiggles so wiggle with me!

Point to self.
Hop up and down.
Flip-flop hands like ears.
Pretend to wag tail.
Wiggle nose.

Jill Coakley—Three-Year-Olds
Generations Childcare
Rochester, NY

Old MacDonald Had a Song

If "Old MacDonald" is one of your class favorites, make these nesting cans for use when the group sings the song. Collect a number of cans that are different sizes. Cover the rims of the cleaned cans with tape. Next, cover each can with Con-Tact paper; then attach a picture of a different farm animal to each can. Label the cans. When you're ready to sing, stack the cans inside one another. At the beginning of each verse, have a child pull out the center can to indicate which animal to sing about next. Later, put the cans in a music or games center. Sequencing skills are improved with a song!

Patti Moeser—Toddlers/Preschool, U. W. Madison Preschool Lab, Madison, WI

Hoe! Hoe! Hoe!

(sung to the tune of "Row, Row, Row Your Boat")

Hoe, hoe, hoe your garden
Up and down the rows.
See the [sun] come [shining down] and watch your garden grow!

Repeat the song, replacing the underlined words with rain *and* pouring down.

Frances Easterling, Magee, MS

A Song for Mothers

This tribute to mothers will have youngsters singing *and* spelling!

(sung to the tune of "Oscar Mayer Weiner Song")

Oh, my mother has a special name.
It's M-O-M-M-Y!
My mother has a special name.
It's M-O-M-M-Y!
Oh, I love to hug her every day.
And when I kiss her, I will say,
"Mommy, mommy, I love you!
I L-O-V-E Y-O-U!"

Laureen Schroeder—Pre-K Special Education, Deltona Lakes Elementary
Deltona, FL

Happy Trails

(sung to the tune of "Happy Trails to You")

Happy trails to you,
It's the end of our school year.
Happy trails to you,
Now summertime is here.
Next year we'll be in kindergarten,
But pre-k's the grade we left our heart in.
Happy trails to you,
It's time to say, "So long!"

Rhonda Leigh Dominguez
Oconee Pre-K at Downs Preschool
Bishop, GA

A Song for the Seashore

Did you know that a trip to the beach can be a stimulating experience for all five senses? This song will help your youngsters remember just how "sense-ational" the seashore is!

(sung to the tune of "Do Your Ears Hang Low?")

Feel sand in my toes.
Smell the ocean with my nose.
See the children splash and play
On a hot summer day.
Hear the ocean waves go ROAR
As they crash into the shore.
Taste the salty sea.

Karen Briggs—Preschool, Marlborough Early Childhood Center
Marlborough, MA

Hooray for the USA!

Hip, hip, hooray! Your preschoolers are sure to feel patriotic when you teach them this Independence Day ditty!

(sung to the tune of "This Old Man")

USA! USA!
Say hooray for the USA!
On this fourth day of July,
Hold your head up high,
And say hooray for the USA!

LeeAnn Collins—Director, Sunshine House Preschool, Lansing, MI

Fingerplays, Poems, & Rhymes

Tiny Apple Seed

After teaching youngsters this poem, put some apple seeds in a container at your sand center so that students can "plant" them under the ground.

I put a tiny apple seed

Underneath the ground.

I covered it with soft, brown dirt;

Then patted all around.

The sun shone down; the rain fell too,

Upon my seed, you see.

And now my tiny apple seed

Is a big apple tree!

Deborah Garmon, Groton, CT

Poems, & Rhymes

Turkey Countdown

Invite ten children to stand in a row and pretend to be turkeys. (Be sure to encourage plenty of wing-flapping and gobbling from your little actors!) As a group, recite the following rhyme; then have the turkeys quickly trot off one by one as you count them down.

Ten fat turkeys, standing in a row.
They spread their wings and tails just so.
They look to the left;
Then they look to the right.
When they strut their stuff, they're quite a sight!
But you won't see them on Thanksgiving Day
'Cause one by one they'll run away! Ten, nine, eight…

Counting Cookies

Your little ones are sure to enjoy this sweet cookie countdown. With each consecutive verse another cookie disappears! To extend the learning opportunities, create flannelboard cookie pieces and a reindeer sock puppet for students to use as they recite the poem.

[Five] little cookies sitting on a plate
Waiting for Santa—
He was running late!
Along came a reindeer,
Guess what he ate…
Crunch!

[Four] little cookies sitting on a plate…

Merrilee Walker
Richmond, RI

Hearts in Hands

   After youngsters learn this fingerplay, they'll want to make heaps of hearts! So follow up the fingerplay by providing a variety of materials such as pipe cleaners, thin strips of paper, and glue sticks. Then lead youngsters to discover that this heart poem works for making all kinds of hearts!

Now's the time to make a heart.

Form a V—it's the place to start.

A big hump on one side,

And now another.

This heart shows the love we have for each other!

LeeAnn Collins—Director
Sunshine House Preschool
Lansing, MI

Five Little Leprechauns

Five little leprechauns, playing in the sun.

The first one said, "Oh, my! We're having fun!"

The second one said, "We need to spread some joy!"

The third one said, "Let's find some girls and boys."

The fourth one said, "There's gold to be found!"

The fifth one said, "Let's look all around!"

Then out came a rainbow, shining bright and bold.

So five little leprechauns ran to find some gold!

adapted from a poem by
April Lena Pace—Three- and Four-Year-Olds
Suffolk Kids Cottage
Brentwood, NY

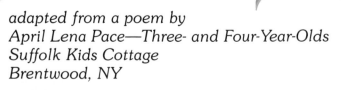

Fuzzy Wuzzy Caterpillar

Your classroom will be bursting with butterflies when youngsters perform this action poem!

Fuzzy wuzzy caterpillar crawls along the ground.

Eating lots of grass and leaves,

He soon grows big and round!

He builds a house around himself.

Now can you tell me why?

'Cause soon you'll see him turn into

A pretty butterfly!

Cele McCloskey and Brenda Peters
Head Start of York County
York, PA

Picnic in the Park

Feel like having a summertime picnic? You will after teaching youngsters this poem!

Summer is the right time
To picnic in the park.
Let's eat lots of food
And stay out until dark!
Hamburgers and hot dogs
On the barbecue,
Corn and beans and pickles,
Potato salad too!
When our plates are empty,
We'll have something sweet—
Juicy watermelon!
What a picnic treat!

Lucia Kemp Henry

It's Circle Time

Gingerbread Men on the Loose

Introduce your new preschoolers to your classroom centers with a treasure hunt involving that storybook favorite, the Gingerbread Man. To prepare the hunt, cut several small gingerbread men from construction paper. Write a clue on each cutout and place each one in an area of your classroom you'd like to introduce to your new students. At circle time, read aloud your favorite version of *The Gingerbread Man.* Then act surprised as you find the first note at the back of the book. It might read, "Look in the housekeeping area under the sink." Send a pair of children to that center, where they'll find the next note directing children's attention to another center. End your treasure hunt with a final clue that leads to a hidden stash of *real* gingerbread men for everyone to enjoy!

JaneLee Dozier—Four- and Five-Year-Olds
Goodpasture Christian School, Madison, TN

Look in the sand table.

Musical Names

This twist on Musical Chairs will help your youngsters recognize their names! First, print each child's name on a separate index card. Then place a class supply of chairs in a circle and put a name card on each chair. Play recorded music and have youngsters walk around the circle of chairs. When the music stops, have each child find the chair with her name, pick up the card, and sit down. Then switch the cards to different chairs, restart the music, and play again! No losers—just winners in *this* name game!

Dorothy Hso—Four- and Five-Year-Olds
Grace Brethren Preschool
Westerville, OH

Space Walk

If you're planning a space theme, this group activity will be astronaut-appropriate! Spread out a playground parachute and have little ones sit around it and hold its edge. Toss some inflatable beach balls or globes onto the parachute to serve as moons and planets. Then have a child take a turn walking, crawling, dancing, or hopping around the bouncing heavenly bodies as the remaining children shake the parachute to the beat of some lively music.

Lori Alisa Burrow—Preschool, Our Town Playschool, Yuba City, CA

Where's That Worm?

Combine rhyme and numbers in this seasonal group activity. To prepare, cut ten apple shapes from red construction paper. Label each apple with a numeral from 1 to 10. Tape a craft stick handle to each apple. Then tape a two-inch-long piece of green pipe cleaner (a worm) to the back of one apple.

At circle time, have ten children stand in front of the class and give each one an apple cutout. Have students recite the following poem; then have a child try to find the worm by naming a numbered apple. Direct the child holding that apple to answer yes or no and show the back of it. Continue the activity until a child finds the worm. Then collect the apples, move the worm, and play the game again.

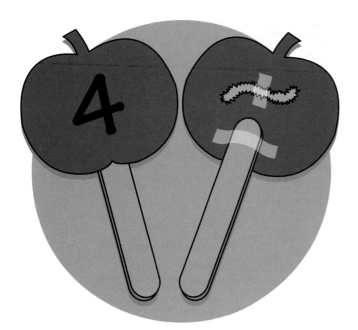

> Ten red apples growing on a tree—
> Five for you and five for me.
> There's one little worm that you can't see.
> Where, oh, where can that little worm be?

Julie Christensen
Littleton, CO

A Friendly Tune

Encourage your preschoolers to find some new friends as they sing this circle-time tune! Have students stand in a circle with one child in the center. Sing the song below, inserting the center child's name where indicated. Have the child choose a classmate from the circle to come to the center with him. Then sing about the chosen child and have her choose another child to enter the center of the circle. When everyone is in a big group and the circle disappears, sing the song again, substituting the word *everyone* for a child's name.

(sung to the tune of "The Farmer in the Dell")

[Child's name] has a friend.
[Child's name] has a friend.
Heigh-ho at [your school's name],
[Child's name] has a friend!

Beth Lemke—PreK
Highland Headstart
Coon Rapids, MN

You've Got Mail!

Get everyone's stamp of approval by using a full-size mailbox in your circle area to introduce each day's group-time topic or activity! Each day before group time, put a different item in the mailbox and raise the flag. For example, you might include an item that will initiate discussion, such as a gourd or Indian corn. Or put in special manipulatives, such as spider rings, that will be used for a game. You could even put the day's story or a snack treat in the box. No matter what you "send" to your class, this idea really delivers!

Charlotte Gardner—Preschool
Shelby County Preschool
Shelbyville, KY

Scurrying Squirrels

Your little ones will go nuts over this autumn adaptation of "Doggy, Doggy, Where's Your Bone?" In advance, make a squirrel headband by gluing two construction paper ears to a tagboard strip. To begin the activity, choose one child to be the squirrel and have him wear the headband. Direct him to leave the circle and cover his eyes. While his eyes are covered, secretly give another child a large pom-pom (nut) to hide in her lap. Signal the squirrel to turn around by having the class chant, "Little squirrel, little squirrel, want a treat? Find the nut for you to eat!" Then have the squirrel find the nut by asking each child, "Do you have a treat?" After he finds the nut, play the game again with a different squirrel.

Boo!

To prepare for this group game, make a class supply of the monster mat on page 38. If desired, color the monsters as shown and then laminate the mats for durability. Provide each child with a mat and five Keebler RAINBOW Vanilla Wafers in a random assortment of colors. To play the game, pull a wafer out of the box and identify the color. If a child has a wafer in that color, she places it on one of the circles on the mat. If she has more than one wafer in that color, she chooses one to place on the mat. Continue calling out colors in this manner. When a child has placed all of her wafers on her mat, she says "Boo!" to signal that her mat is complete. She identifies the colors of her wafers and then everyone eats up!

adapted from an idea by
Roxanne Dearman
North Carolina School for the Deaf
Charlotte, NC

Living Christmas Trees

Need a little Christmas? Right this very minute? Bring on the holiday spirit with this tree trimming idea! In advance, gather various types of old garland. Then prepare a star headband. Also cut out a large supply of tagboard ornament shapes. Invite your little ones to use craft supplies to decorate the ornaments. Then punch a hole in the top of each ornament and attach a yarn loop for hanging. To do this activity, have a child don the star headband and pretend to be a Christmas tree. Then invite the remaining students to use the decorations to trim this little living tree. When the child is fully decorated, take a photo of the results; then remove the decorations. Repeat this process until each child has had a chance to be a Christmas tree.

Cindy Bormann—Three- to Six-Year-Olds
Small World Preschool
West Bend, IA

What's Missing?

Whether you're celebrating Kwanzaa, Hanukkah, or Christmas, this circle-time idea fits the bill! In advance, gather several small items related to the holiday of your choice. For example, use a dreidel, a box wrapped in Hanukkah paper, a Hanukkah card, and a piece of chocolate gelt. Show each item to your youngsters and then place them inside a box. Next, remove all but one of the items from the box. Can your little ones identify which one is missing?

Let It Snow! Let It Snow! Let It Snow!

Put on some lively holiday music and get ready to rev up youngsters' motor skills! Have students hold the edges of a parachute. Open two bags of cotton balls and toss them into the center of the parachute to represent snow. Play upbeat musical selections such as "Let It Snow!" Have students vigorously shake the parachute to send the "snow" flying. It's beginning to look a lot like Christmas!

Lisa Waechter—Preschool
YMCA Cedear Lake Child Care Center
West Bend, WI

Shadow Search

Your little groundhogs will love this shadow-searching game. To prepare, cut out a groundhog shape from black construction paper to represent the groundhog's shadow. Seat youngsters in a circle and choose one child to be the groundhog. Have him crouch away from the circle and close his eyes. Next, have another child hide the groundhog shadow in the room. Ask her to leave a small portion of the shadow visible so that it can be found easily. Have the children call the groundhog back to the group by chanting, "Groundhog, groundhog, where'd you go? Come and find your own shadow!" Direct the groundhog to search around the room and find the shadow. What a fun way to sharpen youngsters' visual acuity!

Pat Bennett—Two-, Three-, and Four-Year-Olds
Young Environment Child Care Center
Erie, PA

Flossing Fun

Just how does flossing work? Help little ones understand with this circle-time idea. All you need to get started is a long piece of cloth, such as a bathrobe belt, to simulate a piece of floss. Then, during group time, invite a small group of youngsters to form a line to represent a row of teeth. Ask the children to stand close together with their hands at their sides. Have two children hold the ends of the floss; then have them work together to gently guide the floss in an up and down motion between the teeth. Be sure to give every child a chance to floss these pearly whites. Oh, my! There's a whole lot of flossing going on!

Karen Palmer—Four- and Five-Year-Olds
Stringfellow School
Coppell, TX

Easter Egg Roll

You'll have group-time giggles when your little ones try this game! To prepare, half-fill a plastic Easter egg with sand. Seal the egg shut with tape or hot glue. Have your preschoolers sit in a circle; hand the egg to one child. Have that child say a classmate's name and try to roll the egg to that person. The child who receives the egg then calls another name and makes an attempt to roll the egg. Keep the pace quick and little ones will be laughing at this egg with a mind of its own!

Susan Pufall—Three-Year-Olds
Red Cliff Early Head Start
Bayfield, WI

Seed-Packet Lotto

Studying about seeds and plants? Use real seed packets to create this fun lotto game! Purchase a number of seed packets for familiar fruits, vegetables, and flowers. Make color copies of the packet covers; then glue the copies onto sheets of construction paper to create different gameboards. If desired, laminate the boards for durability. Use the original seed packets (or full-size copies) as calling cards for the game and use seed cutouts for markers.

Sharon Bailey—PreK
E.O.P.A. Toledo Head Start
Toledo, OH

Read-and-Tell

Promote literacy skills and a love of books by using this variation of show-and-tell. In advance, ask a child to bring her favorite book on her designated read-and-tell day. During circle time, have the child share her book with the group. If the child needs prompting, you might ask her about the cover, her favorite page, and the story's ending or beginning. If the child is already familiar with her book, then have her "read" the story to her preschool friends. For a child who does not bring a book on her special reading day, consider having her choose a familiar classroom favorite; then spend a few moments helping her prepare for her reading.

Mary Epthimiatos
P.S. 180
Brooklyn, NY

Spin the Watermelon

Here's a fresh-off-the-vine idea for a summer circle time! Seat your class in a circle; then put an oblong-shaped watermelon on the floor in the center of the circle. Use a permanent marker to draw a face on one end of the watermelon. To play, invite a child to give the watermelon a spin. Invite the group to join in as you sing the song below. When the watermelon stops, the child at whom it is facing gets to take the next turn spinning the watermelon. Play the game, for several days if necessary, until every child has had an opportunity to spin the watermelon. Then slice the watermelon and give everyone a chance to eat it!

(sung to the tune of "Pease Porridge Hot")

Watermelon red, watermelon green,
Spin that watermelon so it smiles at me!

Patricia Duncan—Pre-K
American School for the Deaf
West Hartford, CT

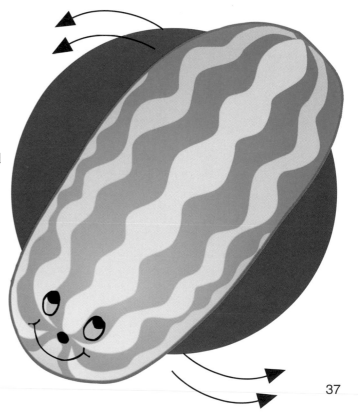

Monster Mat
Use with "Boo!" on page 34.

Get Moving!

Movement Ideas for Preschoolers

Get Moving!

Movement Ideas for Preschoolers

Leaves Everywhere!

Pile on the fun when you invite youngsters to play in some realistic-looking leaves! To make leaves, crinkle and then flatten sheets of tissue paper. Laminate the sheets before cutting out leaf shapes. Make a big pile of paper leaves; then give directions for a movement—such as shuffle, hop, jump, or toss—for each child to perform on her turn to move through the pile. Then focus on body parts with the following song. Have youngsters place one or two paper leaves on each body part as it's sung. At the end, have little ones grab leaves from the ground and toss them into the air!

(sung to the tune of "Twinkle, Twinkle, Little Star")

Leaves, leaves, everywhere—
On my hands, my feet, my hair!
On my shoulders, on my toes,
One right here upon my nose!
Leaves, leaves, everywhere—
On the ground and in the air!

Christy Thomas—Preschool
Southern Baptist Theological Seminary CDC
Louisville, KY

Step Right Up!

This sensory stomp is a real crowd pleaser! To prepare, gather three small plastic wading pools, or cut three large boxes so that the sides are approximately one foot high. Fill one pool with shredded newspaper, one with foam packing material, and one with large bubble wrap. Divide your class into three small groups and have each group stand in a different pool. Next, play some lively music and encourage each group to stomp through the material in the pool. Stop the music. Have the groups switch pools; then begin the activity again. If necessary, replenish the bubble wrap in the pool before repeating the activity. To add a seasonal twist, play a musical selection such as "Monster Mash" and encourage youngsters to move like monsters through the pools.

Lori Burrow
Meridian, CA

Skating Spree

Youngsters will feel like stars on ice with this movement activity! Have students remove their shoes and stand in a circle in an uncarpeted area. Begin playing some lively music and invite them to skate in their socks around the circle. Periodically stop the music and direct your little skaters to stop and take a bow. Resume playing the music and instruct your youngsters to continue skating—in the opposite direction! Continue the activity in this manner, giving your preschoolers plenty of practice skating in clockwise and counterclockwise directions.

LeeAnn Collins—PreK
Sunshine House Preschool
Lansing, MI

Santa Song

Santa's coming to town and he's ready to get moving! Invite each child to pretend that she is clothed in Santa's garb. Then encourage children to sing the song below with motions. If desired, increase the speed of the song each time you repeat it.

*(sung to the tune of
"Head, Shoulders, Knees, and Toes")*

Hat, whiskers, belt, and boots, belt and boots.
Hat, whiskers, belt, and boots, belt and boots.
Twinkling eyes and a little cherry nose.
Hat, whiskers, belt, and boots, belt and boots.

Donna Selling—Four-Year-Olds
First Presbyterian Preschool
Waynesboro, VA

belt and boots...

It's Cold Outside!

Button up your overcoat 'cause it's *cold* outside! As you sing the song below, encourage children to join in with you and add their own original motions.

(sung to the tune of "The Farmer in the Dell")

Let's put on our coats.
Let's put on our coats.
Let's put on our coats today.
It's cold outside!

Let's button and zip our coats.
Let's button and zip our coats.
Let's button and zip our coats today.
It's cold outside!

Let's put on our hats.
Let's put on our hats.
Let's put on our hats today.
It's cold outside!

adapted from an idea by Cris Edwards—Three-Year-Olds
Helena United Methodist Church
Helena, AL

Let's put on our mittens...

Rockin' and Rollin'

Even your shyest preschooler will want to move to the music with this idea! Collect a new colorful flyswatter for each child in your class. Demonstrate how to use the swatter as a pretend guitar. Play an upbeat musical selection such as Greg and Steve's "ABC Rock" or "The Number Rock." Then invite your youngsters to strum their guitars and move to the beat of the music. Have students play their flyswatter guitars often. By the end of the school year, you might want to include a lively number for them to perform during a program. Come on, everyone! Let's rock!

Kris Kelly—Preschool
Country Kids Preschool
Spanish Fork, UT

Stuck on You!

Little feet will be tickled with this sticky sensory experience! Tape strips of duct tape (adhesive side out) around each child's shoes as shown. Play a lively musical selection and invite your youngsters to move to the music. Your preschoolers will enjoy not only the feel of the tape but also the sticky sound it makes as it comes off the floor.

Peggy Wieck—PreK, Litchfield Prekindergarten, Litchfield, IL

Roll 'em, Roll 'em, Roll 'Em

Burritos, anyone? Combine dramatic play and movement with a small-group activity that just might make little ones hungry. Have each child in turn lie on a small blanket on the floor. Pretend to sprinkle cheese, lettuce, and tomatoes over him. Then have the child roll over and over as another child wraps the blanket around him, creating a pretend burrito. One burrito, coming up!

Cindy Farnham—Three- and Four-Year-Olds
Boothbay Head Start
Boothbay, ME

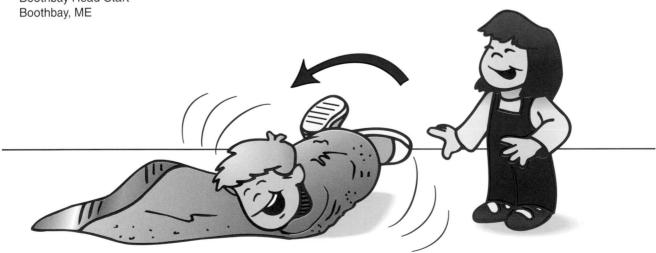

It's Raining! It's Pouring!

Get ready for a shower of giggles with this springtime movement activity! In advance, scatter pretend raindrops (foam packing pieces) over your circle-time area. Invite youngsters to the area. Begin singing the song shown and have youngsters slowly toss the foam pieces into the air to create a pretend sprinkling of rain. Sing each verse faster and faster and have students toss the raindrops in time to the music. Before long, you'll have a downpour of rain and movement fun!

(sung to the tune of "Are You Sleeping?")

It is [sprinkling].
It is [sprinkling].
Drip, drop, drip.
Drip, drop, drip.

Rain is [slowly] falling.
Rain is [slowly] falling.
Drip, drop, drip.
Drip, drop, drip.

Sing a second verse, replacing the underlined words with showering *and* quickly. *Then sing the final verse below.*

It is pouring!
It is pouring!
Splash, splash, splash!
Splash, splash, splash!

Rain is all around us!
Rain is all around us!
Splash, splash, splash!
Splash, splash, splash!

Hoop Passing

This circle activity is all about cooperation and friendship! Ask your group to form a circle and hold hands. Place a plastic hoop over one child's arm. Tell youngsters that the object of this activity is to pass the hoop around the circle without letting go of one another's hands. Guide the first child to step into the hoop with one foot, duck his head and shoulders into the hoop, and then step through the hoop with his other foot so that the hoop ends up on his other arm. Go around the circle once to allow each child to practice this maneuver. Then play some lively music and let the hoop passing begin! Stop the music and name the child who has the hoop at that moment. Then have youngsters chant the rhyme below. Start the music and the hoop passing again, stopping the next time for another child. Continue until you've stopped the music and chanted about each child.

Hoop-dee-hoop-dee-hoop-dee-doo!
[Child's name], [child's name], we like you!

adapted from an idea by Amy Reynolds—Four-Year-Olds
Merry Moppet Preschool
Belmont, CA

BUSY HANDS

Creative Learning Experiences
for Little Hands

BUSY HANDS

Creative Learning Experiences for Little Hands

FLUFF AND STUFF

These free-exploration activities invite your children to have fun with things that are fluffy!

by Michele M. Stoffel Menzel

POOFY PAINTINGS!

Have young artists make poofy paintings with a traditional favorite—tinted shaving cream! Simply squirt several mounds of shaving cream and different colors of food coloring inside the paint tray at the bottom of your easel. When one of your artists visits this center, provide him with a soft nylon shower puff and a squeegee. Encourage him to use the puff to paint a shaving cream design on the easel. Then, when he finishes painting, have him squeegee the shaving cream toward the paint tray for easy cleanup!

A CHANCE FOR CLOUDS

Today's forecast calls for clouds mixed with kids having fun! Simply scatter mounds of Poly-Fil stuffing throughout your classroom. Invite children to look for these Poly-Fil clouds. Have them jump over and around the clouds; then encourage them to gather their clouds and explore the puffiness. For a special touch, have youngsters combine their puffs to form a giant cloud! Wow! It's definitely cloudy now!

STICK 'EM ON

Patterning fun is so easy! Just scatter a number of cotton balls and cotton swabs on the floor of your class-room. Then give each child a 12-inch piece of clear tape or masking tape. Invite her to collect as many balls and swabs as she can, attaching them to her tape in a pattern. Ready? Set? Stick 'em on!

POM-POM PLAY

If you've got a stockpile of pom-poms readily available, provide hours of fun using this simple idea! Simply add pom-poms to your empty sand and water tables along with scoops and pails. Also add containers with different-size holes cut out of their bottoms. As children scoop and sift the pom-poms, encourage them to sort them into the containers and count and pattern them. It's a great day for pom-pom play!

BUSY HANDS

Creative Learning Experiences for Little Hands

STRINGS AND THINGS

ideas contributed by Lisa Leonardi, Jumpstart for Juniors, Norfolk, MA

LOVE TO LACE!

Sheets of plastic canvas make super sturdy lacing cards. Cut thin plastic lacing into long lengths; then knot one end of each length. Invite a youngster to weave the plastic lacing in and out of the holes in the plastic canvas to make a design of his choice. Or use a permanent marker to draw (or trace) a simple shape onto a sheet of plastic canvas; then encourage a child to lace along the outline.

FUNNY FACES

Put smiles on your students' faces with this fun felt activity. Cut various colors of felt into large circles and ovals. Then cut colorful yarn or pipe cleaners into various lengths. Invite a child to choose a felt "face" and then shape features for it from the yarn or pipe cleaner pieces.

As a seasonal variation, cut orange felt pumpkin shapes and provide black yarn or pipe cleaner lengths. What jolly jack-o'-lanterns!

SPAGHETTI STATION

Serve up some fun with this water-table activity. To prepare, cut foot-long lengths of string, yarn, curling ribbon, and plastic lacing. Place them in your water table, along with pasta forks and colanders. Then invite little ones to stir, scoop, sift, and further explore the wet strings and things.

WEAVE IT

Make a few of these weaving trays to get lots of little hands busy with a weaving workout. To make one, use a pencil to poke an equal number of evenly spaced holes along two opposite sides of a foam vegetable tray. Knot one end of a 36-inch length of yarn to a corner hole on the tray. Thread the yarn through the holes, making rows; then knot the loose end to the last hole. Provide several lengths of yarn, ribbon, string, or twine in different colors. Invite a child to weave the strings and things over and under the rows on the tray. When she's finished, she can save her work or remove the strings to prepare the tray for the next child who is wigglin' to weave.

BUSY HANDS

Creative Learning Experiences for Little Hands

CHILL OUT!

Keep little hands busy with these really cool and creative activities!

ideas contributed by Kathy H. Lee—Early Childhood Facilitator, Alpharetta, GA

SNOW CAPS

There's "snow" way your little ones will miss the chance to make snowball look-alikes at this sensory center. Combine enough grated Ivory soap, torn white toilet paper, and cold water in a sensory tub to make a gooey mixture that can be shaped into messy mounds Youngsters are sure to have a ball!

THE DEEP FREEZE

Ask your children to help you place small plastic fish or arctic animal toys into a number of resealable plastic bags. Next have the students help you fill the bags with blue water. Seal the bags; then put them in the freezer overnight. Ask the children to predict what will happen. The next day, ask them to describe how the bags look different. What happened to the toys? Place the bags in a science center for observation throughout the day.

POPSICLE PAINTBRUSHES

To prepare for this cool creative experience, fill shaker containers (such as salt shakers or spice containers) with powdered tempera paint. Next, fill ice cube trays with water. Cover the trays with aluminum foil; then insert a Popsicle stick into each section of each tray. When the water is frozen, remove the cubes from the tray. Encourage a child to shake some paint onto white construction paper and then to use the Popsicle paintbrushes to turn the powder into a painting.

FUN CUBED

The fun just multiplies with this sensory activity. Fill regular or shaped ice cube trays with colored water; then put them in the freezer. Put the ice into a sensory tub along with measuring cups, bowls, spoons, tongs, and other items that the children can use to explore the melting cubes and cold water.

BUSY HANDS

Creative Learning Experiences
for Little Hands

COLOR CONNECTIONS

RAIN MAKES RAINBOWS

Have a child arrange various colors of shredded tissue paper onto a white paper plate. Then invite the child to use a spray bottle filled with water to wet the paper. The colors from the tissue paper will transfer onto the plate, leaving behind a beautiful print when the papers are removed.

ROLLING RAINBOWS

To make a rolling rainbow for your little ones' enjoyment, fill a large clear plastic soft drink bottle with water and colorful plastic mosaic tiles (found in craft stores with the supplies for mosaic projects). Seal the cap tightly, adding a bit of hot glue for protection against leaks. Give it a roll and watch the colors whirl!

SIFT AND SORT

Add colorful pom-poms to your sensory table sand. Encourage children to use slotted spoons and sifters to find the pom-poms. Then challenge them to sort the pom-poms by color. For even more fun, help them arrange the pom-poms in rows to resemble a rainbow.

LET'S COLLABORATE!

In this activity, three colors *and* two artists are better than one! Gather red, yellow, and blue tempera paint; then put a small amount of each on separate trays. Add small rollers to the paint and provide a big piece of paper or tagboard for each pair of painters. Invite two children to paint, and it won't be long before rainbows appear!

BUSY HANDS

Creative Learning Experiences for Little Hands

METALLIC MAGIC

Keep little hands busy with these shiny and reflective ideas.

by Michele M. Stoffel Menzel

FUN FOIL

Little ones will have a ball with this recycled foil idea. In advance, have children bring clean, recycled aluminum foil from home. To make a ball, begin by having a child form a piece of foil into a ball shape. Have children add more foil pieces, continuing this layering process until the ball has reached the desired size. Then invite children to roll, catch, or toss this shiny toy!

SLEEK DIGS

Brighten up your dramatic-play area with this sleek hideout. Place a refrigerator box on its side. With a utility knife, remove one of the long panels to create an opening. Invite children to assist you in taping lengths of foil to the inside walls and floor. Decorate the opening with strips of silver garland. Store some flashlights inside the box. Then encourage little ones to use the flashlights to explore these shiny new digs!

RIPPLIN' REFLECTIONS

Make some waves at your water table with all that glitters and gleams. Line your empty table with aluminum foil; then fill it with water. Add your favorite shiny or reflective materials including lengths of garland or pieces of shiny mylar paper. Then provide flashlights and handheld mirrors. Encourage children to use their hands to make waves in the water. Then invite them to use the flashlights to shine light into the water and onto the mirrors to reflect the light of the metallic objects. How's that for some ripplin' fun?

Learning Centers

Oodles of Noodles

The end of summer means you'll be able to find plenty of swim noodles on sale, so stock up! Cut the foam noodles into one-inch pieces and encourage youngsters to thread them onto yarn lengths to create colorful necklaces. Have older preschoolers practice patterning skills as they create necklaces with color patterns. Or have little ones stack the noodle pieces into towers, toss them at targets, or sort them by color in your water table. However you use them, they'll be oodles of fun!

Amy Rain Monahan—Three-Year-Olds
Saint Anthony's Wellness Center Play Pals
Alton, IL

Lorraine Bretzman—Preschool
Peru YMCA Preschool
Peru, IN

That's Me!

Bring some friendly faces to your block center when you make these fun photo cylinders! To make one, take a full-body photograph of a child; then cut out the child's body from the developed photo. Next, cover a cardboard tube with construction paper or colored Con-Tact paper. Glue the cutout photo to the toilet paper tube; then cover the tube with a strip of clear Con-Tact paper for durability. Place each child's cylinder in the block center and invite your preschoolers to build structures for these familiar faces.

Dayle Timmons
Jacksonville Beach, FL

Octopus and Starfish Arms

Once they dive in, your students are sure to get stuck on this center! Obtain a rubber bath mat that has small suction cups on one side. Cut it into starfish shapes and strips (to resemble octopus arms). Add the shapes and strips to your water table. As students have fun experimenting with the suction cups, they'll learn how octopi and starfish move about and cling to objects. Don't be surprised if parents report that youngsters want to try this ocean critter idea with bath mats at home, too!

Dina Fehler—Preschool
Kirkland, WA

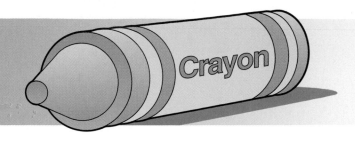

Fishing for Friends

Help your new preschoolers get to know their classmates with this fun fishing game! To prepare, collect two juice can lids for each child. Take a head-and-shoulders photo of each child; then get double prints made. Cut the photos to fit the juice can lids and glue them in place. Lay all the lids facedown on the floor in the center. Then provide a child or group at this center with a fishing pole made from a wooden dowel or yardstick, a length of string, and a magnet. Have each child try to "catch" two matching lids and identify the child pictured on them. If you're fishing for a way to store this game, just stack the lids inside a potato chip canister!

Cindy Bormann—Preschool
Small World Preschool
West Bend, IA

Roll Me a Letter!

Youngsters will be on a roll with letter recognition at this painting center. Hot-glue several sturdy foam letters (from craft stores) onto an unopened eight-ounce can of tomato sauce. Set the can in your art center along with paper and shallow pans of tempera paint. To use the center, a child rolls the can in paint and then onto his paper. Encourage him to "read" his printed paper.

Patricia Moeser—Preschool
University of Wisconsin Preschool Lab Site 1
Madison, WI

Pumpkin Pie Play Dough

5½ c. flour
2 c. salt
8 tsp. cream of tartar
¾ c. oil

1 container (1¹⁄₁₂ ounces) pumpkin pie spice
orange food coloring (2 parts yellow, 1 part red)
4 c. water

Mix all of the ingredients together. Cook and stir over medium heat until lumps disappear. Knead the dough on a floured surface until it is smooth. Store in an airtight container.

Jeanette Jonas—Pre-K
Rainbow Child Care Center
Bakersfield, CA

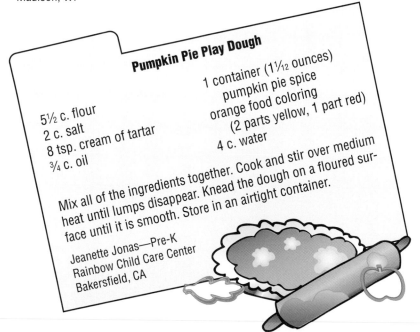

Pumpkin Pie Play Dough

This yummy-smelling dough is sure to add spice to your play-dough area! Place a batch of this scented dough and some white play dough in your center. Add some fall cookie cutters, small pie tins, and rolling pins to the area. Invite your little ones to make fall cookies. Or encourage them to make play-dough pumpkin pies, using the white dough for crust and the scented dough for filling. Encourage your little bakers to make as many pastries as they want, but remind them that these goodies only smell good. No tasting please!

Pick a Patch of *P*s

Get the dirt on this unique sensory experience that reinforces the sound of the letter *P*. Cut out a number of large tagboard seed shapes. Program some of the seeds by attaching stickers or pictures of things that begin with the letter *P*. Put the programmed seeds and the blank seeds in a tub filled with soil or sand. Add a pair of gloves, a plastic shovel, and a pumpkin pail to the area. Invite a child visiting the center to use the shovel to find the programmed seeds and put them in the pumpkin pail. To reinforce his learning, sing the song below with him, substituting the word *pumpkin* with the items on the seeds.

(sung to the tune of "The Farmer in the Dell")

> [Pumpkin] begins with *P*.
> [Pumpkin] begins with *P*.
> \p\ \p\ \p\ \p\ \p\ \p\
> [Pumpkin] begins with *P*.

adapted from an idea by Henry Fergus
Phoenix, AZ

Halloween Tic-Tac-Toe

Your little boys and "ghouls" will love this holiday version of tic-tac-toe! To prepare, purchase or ask parents to donate some paper plates with a Halloween design, as well as two different types of Halloween candies (such as candy corn and holiday M&M's candies). Use a black permanent marker to draw tic-tac-toe grids on a plate. Then use one type of candy for Xs and the other for Os. Provide fresh candy for each game and invite youngsters to eat it afterward. Or keep the candy to be used as playing pieces in a designated bag, and have a separate bowl of treats for snacking.

Sarah Booth—Four- and Five-Year-Olds
Messiah Nursery School
South Williamsport, PA

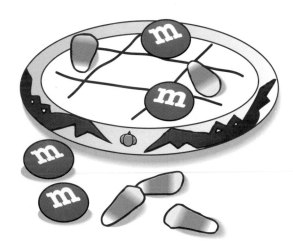

Mr. Pumpkin Head

He's not just a jack-o'-lantern—he's Mr. Pumpkin Head! Try this twist on pumpkin carving this fall season. Place a small to medium-size pumpkin in your fine-motor area. Poke some holes where the eyes, nose, mouth, and other features (such as a hat or ears) should be. Then provide the pieces from a Mr. Potato Head game and invite youngsters to change Mr. Pumpkin Head's appearance daily!

Sheri Dressler—PreK
Woodland School
Carpentersville, IL

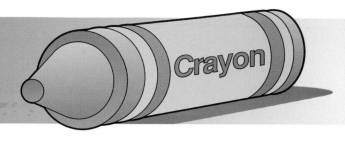

Boo Bowling

Roll into Halloween with a game of Boo Bowling! To make ghostly bowling pins, drape circles cut from an old white sheet over several tall plastic containers, such as those used for powdered coffee creamer. Tie a length of black yarn around the neck of each container to hold the fabric in place; then use a black marker to add eyes. Set the ghost pins in bowling formation; then invite a child to roll a heavy ball toward the pins to try to knock them down.

Jeanie Young—Special Education
Lake Orion Community Schools L.O.O.K. First Program
Lake Orion, MI

A Real Pumpkin Puzzle

Youngsters will be piecing together this pumpkin puzzle again and again when you try this imaginative carving idea! Cut off the top of a large pumpkin and clean the inside as you would for carving a jack-o'-lantern. Next, draw a wavy line all around the pumpkin, about two inches below the cut-off top. Cut on the line; then set aside the resulting ring of pumpkin. Draw a different type of line, such as a zigzag, about two inches from the current top. Cut along that line to create a second pumpkin ring. Keep going, using a unique cut for each layer. Then challenge your students to visit the puzzle area to reassemble the pumpkin by stacking the rings atop one another. Cool!

Marie Drake—Five-Year-Olds
Younger Years, Inc.
Meadville, PA

See the Seeds

Help little ones understand the concept of seeds growing into specific plants with this addition to your discovery area. Gather several packets of vegetable, fruit, and flower seeds. Cut one end off each packet, leaving as much of the front panel picture intact as possible. Pour the seeds from each packet into a separate zippered plastic bag; then slip the open packet into the bag too. Seal the bags and add clear tape to discourage youngsters from dumping the seeds. Place the bags in your discovery area and invite children to examine them. Encourage them to note how the seeds look alike and different. Take seeds from a few of the packages and plant them. Ask youngsters to predict what will happen. Will the plants look like the pictures on the packets?

Meghan Painton—Preschool, Brunswick Head Start, Brunswick, ME

Indoor Ice Blocks

Add some icy excitement to your block center with this idea. To prepare, cut large pieces of foam to resemble blocks of ice. Then place them in your block center along with some plush toy penguins. Have youngsters use the blocks and birds to create a polar paradise. As they do, they'll have the opportunity to problem-solve and develop creative-thinking skills.

Mary Stechman—Three-Year-Olds
Highland Plaza United Methodist Preschool & Kindergarten
Hixson, TN

That's a Match!

Light the way to shape matching with this center idea! Construct a simple menorah from eight toilet tissue tubes and one paper towel tube. Or create a Kwanzaa kinara from seven toilet tissue tubes. Cover each tube with paper; then glue or staple the tubes together side by side (as shown). Next, cut out a yellow construction paper flame for each tube. Be sure the base of each flame is wider than the tube openings. Laminate the flames for durability; then attach a craft stick to the back of each one. Lastly, program each flame and each tube so that you have pairs of shapes.

To use the center, a child "lights" each candle by slipping in the flame that corresponds to the shape on the candle.

Meg Townsend—Three-Year-Olds
Elbow Lane Nursery School
Warrington, PA

A Cookie Sheet Palette

Looking for easy-to-use painting materials? Look in the kitchen! First, fold a few paper towels so that they fit on the bottom of a cookie sheet. Squirt liquid tempera paint in two different (complementary) colors onto the paper towels. Place a sheet of art paper on another cookie sheet. Invite a child at this center to press cookie cutters onto the paint-soaked paper towels and then press them onto the paper to make prints. Encourage her to keep going until she has a whole tray of yummy-looking cookies!

Cynthia Sayman—Toddlers
All My Children Daycare Center
Binghamton, NY

Frosty Friend

Build a blizzard of sequencing and size-seriation skills with this frosty friend. To prepare, stuff three white trash bags with crumpled newspapers to resemble a small, a medium, and a large snowball. Tie a knot in each bag. Next, cut out black construction paper ovals for students to use as facial features and buttons; then attach a small piece of Sticky-Tac to the back of each oval. Place the snowballs and ovals at your center along with a supply of scarves, mittens, and winter hats (at your discretion). Invite each child to don the winter apparel. Then have her roll, stack, and pat the snowballs to form a snowman's body. Have her add the construction paper features and the snowman is complete!

Audrey Englehardt—Early Childhood Education
Meadowbrook Elementary
Moro, IL

Watch Out for Icebergs!

Brrr! Exciting exploration and discoveries await your youngsters when you turn your water table into a pretend icy ocean! Fill a few large bowls with colored water and freeze them. Then remove these frozen icebergs from the bowls and put them in the water in your table. Add some plastic polar animals for a completely cool experience!

Lori Kracoff—Preschool
Curious George Cottage Learning Center
Waterville Valley, NH

Faux Snow

It's white, it's cold…but is it snow? No, but it's a delightful sensory experience for your preschoolers, especially if you live in an area that doesn't see snow in the winter. Squirt some nonmenthol shaving cream into your sensory table. Then add ice cubes and watch little fingers slip and slide through this cold creamy stuff! Encourage youngsters to stack up ice cubes to build snowmen, too.

Paulette Shupack—Preschool
Gregory Gardens Preschool
Pleasant Hill, CA

Giant Conversation Hearts

What Valentine's Day messages do your little ones like? Find out when they make their own giant-size candy conversation hearts! Invite a youngster at your writing center to trace a heart-shaped candy box onto a sheet of pastel construction paper. Post a list of appropriate messages, such as "I love you" and "Be mine," at the center. Have a child copy the message of her choice onto her heart shape before cutting it out. Display all the candy conversation hearts in your classroom or invite each youngster to take hers home to a special valentine!

adapted from an idea by
Susan Bailey—TMD Special Education
Douglas Elementary
Trenton, SC

Match the Hearts

Here's a numeral-matching center perfect for Valentine's Day! From an old deck of playing cards, remove the numbered cards in the heart suit. Cut each card in half crosswise so that its number shows on both halves. Put the cut cards at your math center, and encourage a child to match the halves of each card.

Jennifer Barton, Elizabeth Green School, Newington, CT

Rose Print Bouquets

This center idea is so simple, yet it provides bouquets of painting fun! Simply stock your art area with silk roses and shallow pans of tempera paint. If desired, add a few drops of rose potpourri oil or perfume to the paint. Invite children who visit the center to dip the roses into the paint and then press them onto large sheets of paper to create rose prints. Everything is coming up roses!

Jenny Anderson
Algonquin, IL

Nutritious Sorting

If you're focusing on nutrition, try this sorting activity to help little ones understand the food groups of the Food Guide Pyramid. Bring over the play foods from your housekeeping area; then gather a special container to represent each of the food groups. Provide a new foam tray for meats and proteins, a gallon milk jug (with the top cut off) for dairy foods, a bread basket for grains, a large salad bowl for vegetables and fruits, and a white paper bakery bag for sweets and fats. Explain the container clues; then let the classification begin!

Julie Noble—Preschool, Homeschooler, Sacramento, CA

Telescoping Tubes

A collection of cardboard tubes and small balls will add fun and science to your block center! Gather cardboard tubes in various lengths and widths, including paper towel tubes, gift wrap tubes, mailing tubes—even carpet tubes! Add small bouncing balls, golf balls, and Ping-Pong balls. Then encourage youngsters to place blocks under the tubes and experiment with varying angles as they send balls through them. It's full-tilt fun!

Linda Bille—Three- and Four-Year-Olds, Riviera United Methodist Preschool
Redondo Beach, CA

Hamburgers, Anyone?

Use this idea to transform your dramatic-play area into a fast-food restaurant. In advance, visit a local fast-food restaurant and request donations of paper bags and unused burger boxes or paper wrappers. Next, cut out bun shapes from sponges, and hamburger patty shapes and toppings from craft foam. Place all of the supplies in the center. Then invite youngsters to take turns making burgers. If desired, use your puppet theater to create a drive-thru window for your restaurant. Add a few tricycles and you're ready for business!

Lisa Dukes—Three-Year-Olds
Wee Ones Preschool
Pflugerville, TX

Nancy M. Lotzer
Farmer's Branch, TX

Bugs in the Grass

Grasshoppers, beetles, and ants—oh my! They'll all be hiding in your sensory table when you set it up for a bug hunt your youngsters will love! Fill the table with green plastic grass; then hide an assortment of plastic insects in the grass. Provide magnifying glasses and let the hunt begin!

Jill Bivens—Four- and Five-Year-Olds
Two Rivers Head Start
Aurora, IL

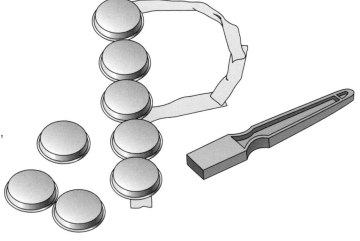

Doughnut Sorting

To prepare for this sweet sorting center, visit a local bakery or doughnut shop and request donations of unused doughnut boxes. Cut a supply of doughnut shapes from craft foam. Next, create different sets of doughnuts by gluing craft-foam frosting or other craft items onto the shapes. Place the doughnuts in a container or on a tray and invite students to sort each set of doughnuts into a different box. One dozen chocolate doughnuts, please!

adapted from an idea by Karen Reed—Four- and Five-Year-Olds
Trailside Daycare, Providence, RI

Juice-Can-Lid Letters

Here's a letter-making activity preschoolers are sure to stick with! Use masking tape to outline letters on the floor or carpet in your literacy center. Add a shoebox filled with metal juice can lids and a magnetic wand. Have a child at this center lay the lids on top of the lines of a letter to trace its shape. When she's done, have her use the magnetic wand to "erase" her work!

Melody Yardley—Two- to Five-Year-Olds
Ms. Peg's Country Care
Odin, IL

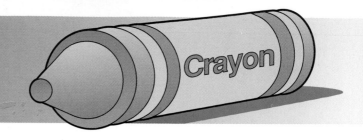

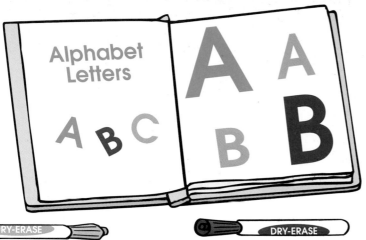

Write 'n' Wipe

Your little ones will make memories as they use this photo album idea to practice their writing skills. Fill the pages of an album that has plastic page protectors with letter-shaped and geometric cutouts. Also fill the pages with cards labeled with students' names. Place the album in your literacy center along with dry-erase markers and tissues. (Slim dry-erase markers are less pungent.) Encourage your little ones to write, wipe, and then write again!

Jenny Unruh—Preschool, Special Education
Georgia Matthews Elementary
Garden City, KS

Digging Up Bones

Youngsters will uncover their archeological skills when digging up these bones. During a study of dinosaurs, hide bone-shaped dog treats in your indoor and outdoor sand centers. Provide youngsters with buckets, shovels, and even paintbrushes to aid them in their digging.

Antares Narizzano—Pre-K
Rainbow Station Child Development Center
Richmond, VA

Underwater World

Use this idea to add some building fun to your water table. To begin, drain the table and let it dry. Then use double-sided tape or loops of masking tape to attach a few DUPLO building bases to the bottom of the table. Fill the table with water; then set a supply of DUPLO pieces near the table. Invite your youngsters to the area to create an underwater wonderland.

Doris Porter—Three- to Five-Year-Olds
Aquin System Preschool, Cascade, IA

Bubble Count

Something's fishy about this math center idea. It's how much fun youngsters have practicing counting and numeral recognition! To prepare the game, cut ten fish shapes from colorful poster board; then write a different numeral from 1 to 10 on each fish. Arrange the fish on a piece of poster board; then trace around them. Use glitter glue to make a different number of bubbles from one to ten above each fish outline. Remove the fish. To use the game, a child counts the number of bubbles above a fish outline. Then he puts the fish with the corresponding numeral on the board beneath the bubbles.

Trish Draper—Pre-K and Gr. K
Millarville Community School
Millarville, Alberta, Canada

How Many Scoops?

Dish up some counting fun with the help of some pretend ice cream! To prepare, write a different numeral from 1 to 10 in the bottom of each of ten foam bowls. Put the bowls in your math center, along with an ice-cream scoop and some play dough balls in a variety of cool and creamy ice-cream colors! Invite a pair of children to visit the center. Have one child choose a bowl and put in the corresponding number of play dough ice-cream scoops. Have him serve it to his partner, who pretends to eat the ice cream while counting to check the server's work. Then have the children switch roles and dish up more fun!

Shelley Banzhaf
Maywood, NE

See the Stars

Create a petite planetarium for your young stargazers! Affix a variety of glow-in-the-dark stickers shaped like stars, moons, and planets to sheets of dark construction paper. Tape the paper to the underside of a table; then cover the table with a dark sheet. Add a few books about space and a couple of flashlights. Then invite your preschoolers to take turns under the table, lying back to look up at the stars and using the flashlights to read all about them!

Rhonda Hixson—Four-Year-Olds
St. Christopher's Center for Children
Vandalia, OH

Getting Your Ducklings in a Row

Getting Your Ducklings

Parent and Child Pictures

At the beginning of the year, do you find it challenging to learn your students' names and match the students with their parents? This idea will make it a snap! When each parent and child arrive on the first day of school, put a nametag on the child; then quickly snap a picture of the child with his parent. After school, have the pictures developed at a one-hour photo lab. Study the pictures that night. The next day you'll be able to call each child by name and when dismissal time arrives, recognizing parents will be quick and easy!

Fran Tortorici—Three-Year-Olds
Castleton Hill Moravian Preschool
Staten Island, NY

Run for the Border

Run to get your next few months' worth of bulletin board border; then make use of this timesaving tip! As you prepare your next bulletin board, choose a neutral background; then layer and attach several borders for future planned displays. For example, mount a Christmas border, then cover it with a Halloween border, and finally top both of those with a fall border. When it's time to change the display, simply peel off the top layer of border. The next border is in place and ready to use!

Amy Barsanti—Four-Year-Olds
St. Andrew's Preschool, Nags Head, NC

Thematic Storage Boxes

Decorate your room and store your teaching materials at the same time. Here's how! Decorate boxes to reflect the thematic materials they will hold. For example, for a farm-related unit, cover a box and its lid with colorful paper. Then glue on farm animal die-cut shapes. Or, for a transportation unit, cover a box with yellow paper. Add black paper wheels, painted windows, and magazine cutout passengers. You'll be able to tell at a glance where your materials for each theme are located. Plus it's a great way to spark youngsters' curiosity for upcoming units!

Amy Aloi and Gwen Blake—Four-Year-Olds
Berkshire Elementary
Forestville, MD

in a Row   Tips For Getting Organized

Mr. Glue, Mr. Scissors, and the Happy Crayons

Introduce your youngsters to these characters and they're sure to remember how to use glue, scissors, and crayons appropriately. To prepare, glue wiggle eyes on a bottle of glue, a pair of scissors, and several crayons. Introduce each character or group of characters individually; then use the characters again whenever a reminder is needed. Here are some things the characters might say to help your children use these art materials.

Teena Perry—Preschool, Rainbow Bears Preschool, Oklahoma City, OK

Mr. Glue: This is my hat (point to orange cap), my head (point to rim of bottle), and my tummy (point to the body of the bottle). To open me, twist my hat this way (demonstrate). I like it when people squeeze my tummy so softly that you can hear and feel me breathe (squeeze the bottle next to each child so he can hear and feel the air going in and out of the bottle). If you squeeze me gently, I will put small drops of glue on your project (demonstrate). Please do not squeeze my tummy too hard. When you are finished, twist my hat back on this way (demonstrate).

The Happy Crayons: The paper wrapped around us keeps us strong. Please do not pull off our papers! Please be careful not to squeeze us too hard or rub us on paper too hard because we might break. Ouch! When you are finished with us, please put us back in our happy home (put crayons back in box or basket) so we do not get lonely or roll away and get lost.

Mr. Scissors: This is my head (point to handle) and this is my mouth (open and close blades). When you carry me, hold my mouth closed so that my teeth don't hurt anyone (demonstrate). If you want to use me, put your thumb in the top of my head and three of your fingers in the bottom of my head (demonstrate). When you are using me to cut, open my mouth wide like this so that I take big bites or open my mouth just a little bit like this so that I take small bites (demonstrate).

Happy Helpers

You'll have lots of happy helpers when you employ this cleanup time management tip! From laminated yellow construction paper, prepare a class supply of smiley faces. Write each child's name on a separate face. To signal that it's time to clean up, hand each child his smiley face. When he has completed his cleaning tasks, have him return it to you. Then use Sticky-Tac adhesive to attach the face to a display titled "Happy Helpers." When your room is clean, everyone will be all smiles!

adapted from an idea by Anita Edlund—Three-Year-Olds
Cokesbury Children's Center, Farragut, TN

Easy Art Easel and Art Display

Got a clip? Use this tip! Use large plastic spring clips (such as those used to clip potato chip bags closed) to create instant easels and displays. Just nail each clip within student reach into a wooden surface, such as a thin piece of plywood, a wall, or the side of a wooden cabinet or shelf. Invite a student to slip a piece of art paper into the clip for an instant easel or hang his work from a clip for display.

Gayle J. Vergara—Preschool
Willowbend Preschool
Murrieta, CA

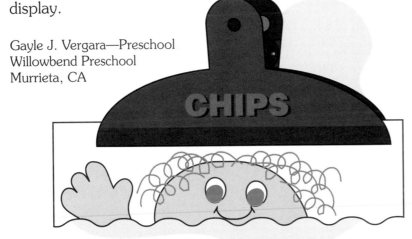

Getting Into Centers

Looking for an easy way to get your preschoolers from group time into centers? Choose a number of items from each center that corresponds to the number of children allowed in the center. For example, if two children can paint at the easel, take two paintbrushes. If four children can go to dramatic play, choose four dress-up items. Place all the representative items on a tray. Call youngsters up one at a time to choose an item from the tray and take it to the chosen center. When the items are gone, the centers are full!

Kellie Kochensparger—Director
Mini University, Inc.—MVH Child Care Center
Dayton, OH

Bulletin Boards by the Book

Can't remember exactly how you made that great bulletin board last year? Avoid the problem by keeping a scrapbook of photos of bulletin boards and displays. Simply take a photo of each board before you take it down. Then compile the photos in a file or scrapbook. You'll never forget, and you'll have a great tool for assistants and parent volunteers when they assemble your displays for you!

Sue Dupree
Gainesville, GA

A Color-Coded Carpet

Guide your preschoolers to your preferred seating arrangements for storytime and group time with the help of colored Velcro fastening tape. Choose one color of Velcro tape and attach strips to your carpet in rows for storytime. Choose another color and attach strips in a circle for group time or show-and-tell. Then just name a color and little ones will know where to sit for the planned activity.

Crystal Young—PreK
Rodriguez School
Austin, TX

No More Lost Notes!

Here's a quick and easy way to send home reminders about important school events. Use a computer to print your reminder on address labels. At the end of the day, peel off the labels and stick each one onto a different child's clothing. Students will love showing off these nifty notes, and parents will be grateful for a reminder that sticks!

Karen Griffin
Cair Paravel–Latin School
Topeka, KS

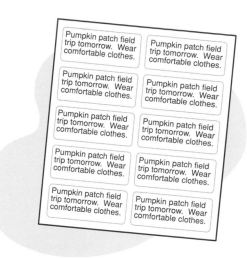

Artsy Envelopes

Share youngsters' artwork with these child-decorated envelopes! Attach blank address labels to a large supply of white envelopes; then place them in your writing center. Invite youngsters to use crayons or water-based markers to decorate the envelopes without coloring the labels. Each time you send home a parent note, just place it inside a decorated envelope. Say, that's an artsy home-school connection right at your fingertips!

Teresa Pearsall—Preschool
Step by Step Childcare Center
Williamston, NC

Recycled Paint Cups

Don't throw away those wonderfully sturdy, plastic frosting containers! They make great paint cups for your easel. To make one, use a craft knife to cut a paintbrush hole in the lid of the container. Then pour paint into the container, snap on the lid, insert the brush, and it's ready for action!

Teresa Edison—Four-
    and Five-Year-Olds
Luther Hospital Child
    Care Center
Eau Claire, WI

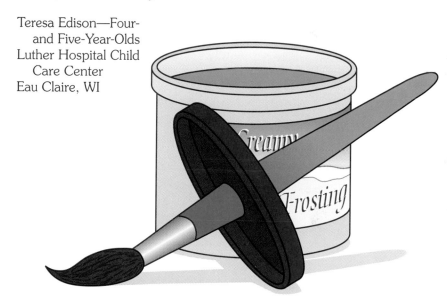

Hold On!

Minimize the mess of painting three-dimensional projects with the help of some well-placed clothespins! Simply clip a wooden clothespin onto the object to be painted; then have the child hold onto the clothespin as she paints the object. Ah…less mess!

Beth Lemke—PreK, Heights Head Start, Columbia Heights, MN

Dish Drainer Book Display

Move a plastic dish drainer from the kitchen to the classroom for this supersimple display idea! Gather books for the season or for your current theme; then stand them up in a dish drainer. They'll be easy to find at storytime or for your preschoolers to flip through during center time. Use the utensil compartment to store bookmarks, too!

Susan Brown—PreK
St. Joseph Early
    Education Center
Shawnee, KS

Smock Frock

Cut back on paint smock expenses with this thrifty idea. To make one, cut out a rectangle from an old vinyl shower curtain or tablecloth. (Adjust the size according to your children's needs.) Then, in the middle of the piece, cut a hole large enough for a child to slip his head through. Keep these smock frocks in your art area where they can easily (and independently!) be slipped on and off.

Peggy L. Emde—Preschool
Kids Under Construction, Inc.
Stillwater, OK

Straw Solution

If your children bring their own snacks or lunches to school, you've probably encountered drink boxes or pouches with missing straws. Keep a supply of coffee-stirring sticks on hand to solve this problem! They're the perfect size to fit drink boxes or pouches, and just as easy to insert as the original straws.

Linda Bille—Three- and Four-Year-Olds
Riviera United Methodist Preschool
Redondo Beach, CA

"So-Easy" Seating

Hey, preschool teachers! Manage your snacktime seating arrangements and teach name recognition at the same time. Here's how! Die-cut a class supply of shapes to reflect your current theme. Place the shapes on the tables so that you have a separate shape for each child. Cover the shapes with clear Con-Tact covering. Then use erasable markers to write a different child's name on each shape. During snacktime, have each child find her seat. After snack, just wipe the tables and the shapes clean. On your marks. Get set. Write! These nifty nametags are ready to use again!

Bobbi Albright—Three- and Four-Year-Olds
Day Care Services of Blair County/Leopold Center
Altoona, PA

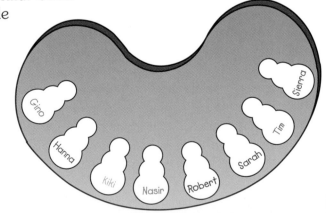

BULLETIN BOARDS AND DISPLAYS

Fishing for Valentines

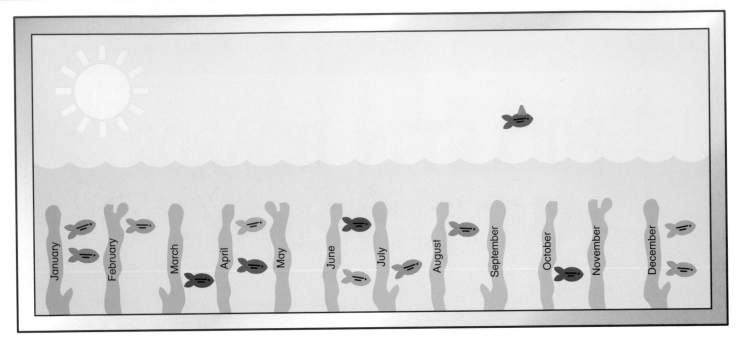

Make a splash with this creative birthday display. Label each of 12 paper seaweed shapes with a different month; then mount them in sequence onto an ocean scene. Have each child decorate a fish cutout labeled with his name and birthday. Use pushpins to display each fish beside the appropriate month. On the day of a child's birthday, display his fish so that it looks as if it is jumping out of the water. If desired, add a party hat cutout to the fish. Happy birthday!

Heather Campbell, Pennington, NJ

Brighten up your classroom with a bulletin board that shows sweet thoughts about new friends. Cut student-fingerpainted paper into circles; then glue a construction paper lollipop stick onto each one. Divide students into pairs. Have each child say something sweet about her partner; then write the sweet statement on her partner's lollipop stick. Mount the completed sweets on a display with a catchy title.

Lori Kent
Hood River, OR

A BLOOMING GARDEN OF ABCs

Aa — ant, animal, apple

Bb — ball, bow, bear

Cc — cap, cake, cat

Dd — dog, doll, duck, dice

Ee — elephant, eraser, egg

Here's a display that blooms as your students' letter recognition grows throughout the year. Along a hallway or on a wide window, mount a paper picket fence and a title. As you study each letter, add a paper flower labeled with that letter to your garden. Invite students to bring in items that begin with the letter. Write the name of each item on a paper leaf to add to the flower's stem. What a way to plant seeds of learning!

Lisa Bigon—Four-Year-Olds, St. Mark Lutheran Preschool, Lake Jackson, TX

This colorful bulletin board is sure to draw a lot of attention. From bulletin board paper, create a large crayon box; then mount it to a bulletin board. Write each child's name in bold letters across a separate large white paper crayon cutout. Have each youngster color his cutout using his favorite crayon color. Mount the crayons around the box; then add a title. For an extra splash of color, surround the board with large inflatable crayons.

adapted from ideas by
Tonie Liddle—Pre-K, Central Baptist Christian
    Academy, Binghamton, NY
Nancy Goldberg—Three-Year-Olds, B'nai Israel
    Schilit Nursery School, Rockville, MD

OUR NEW PACK

Certified Fun

Mrs. Hamrick's Pack 3s

Grant — Janie — Eric — David — Jessy

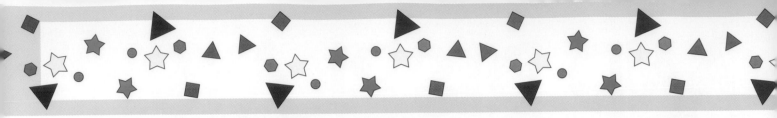

You're sure to get 101 compliments with this dalmatian display! Duplicate the dog pattern (page 82) onto white construction paper for each child. Have a child color and personalize the hat and then press black fingerprints onto the dog. Cut out the pattern. Write a student-given name on the dog tag. In a word balloon, write a fire safety rule dictated by the child. Finally, display the dogs and balloons with a title on a bulletin board.

Lola M. Smith, Hilliard, OH

This seasonal display is a real treat! Have each child paint or color an orange stripe and a yellow stripe across a piece of white paper as shown. When the paint is dry, help each child cut her paper into the shape of a piece of candy corn. Then label the candy corn with the children's names. Display these child-made treats on a bulletin board and then add a title.

Sarah Booth—Four- and Five-Year-Olds
Messiah Nursery School
South Williamsport, PA

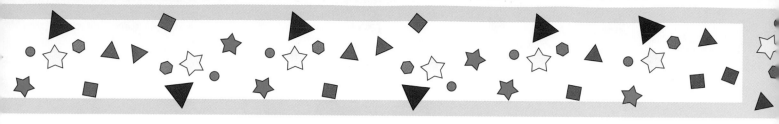

Little ones will wise up to shapes with this owl display. Have each child glue two white circle eyes and an orange triangle beak onto a paper bag. Then have him cover the rest of the bag with yellow rectangle feathers. As a final touch, direct the child to glue on two black circles for pupils and two yellow paper wings. Display the owls on a tree made from crumpled bulletin board paper. Passersby are sure to say, " 'Whooo' made this nice display?"

Barbara Meyers
Fort Worth County Day School
Fort Worth, TX

Here's a turkey that looks too good to eat! To make this display, provide each child with a large poster board feather. Set up a center with a variety of craft items, collage materials, and fingerpaints. Then direct each child to visit the area and decorate his feather as desired. Display the feathers around a large turkey cutout and add a holiday greeting.

Barb Olszewski—Special Education
Elmer Knopf Learning Center
Flint, MI

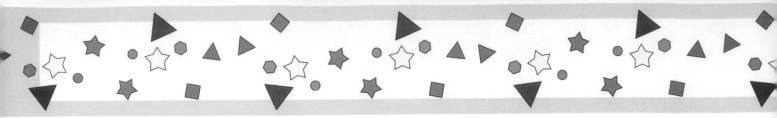

Each of the candles on this menorah will sparkle and glow as you go through the holidays. To create the mosaic-style menorah, have students glue paper pieces onto nine large bulletin board paper rectangles. Mount the pieces on a background. Next, cut out nine more bulletin board paper rectangles to represent the candles. Mount the shammash (central candle) and "light" it with a tissue paper flame. Each day, have students help you add another candle and flame to celebrate.

Nancy Goldberg—Three-Year-Olds, B'nai Israel Schilit Nursery School, Rockville, MD

Invite each child to make an angel for this display. To make one, cut a nine-inch paper plate into four wedge-shaped pieces. Glue together three of the pieces to make the angel's body. To make the angel's arm, cut the fluted border off the fourth piece and then glue the border to the body. Glue a paper circle to the body. Draw facial features on the circle. Staple a length of garland to the head to create a halo; then glue on yarn or raffia for hair. Mount each angel beside a photograph of the child who created it. How heavenly!

Nancy O'Toole—Preschool
Ready, Set, Grow
Grand Rapids, MN

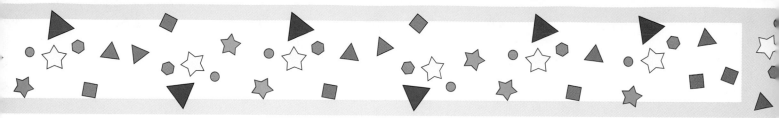

Ms. Tadie's Reindeer

David   Karen   Scott   Misty   Derik   Shawn   Clay   Bonita

This row of reindeer will add some holiday charm to a hallway or your classroom! Paint each child's palm and fingers with brown tempera paint. Have the child press his hand onto a long sheet of bulletin board paper; then write his name under the resulting print. Have students make a row of handprints on the paper. When the prints are dry, invite each child to add construction paper eyes and a pom-pom nose to his print. Label the display to resemble the one shown, and you're ready for a sleigh ride!

Robin Tadie—Preschool, Audubon School, Colorado Springs, CO

To create this display, have each child use paint to make a white footprint on a dark blue sheet of construction paper. When the paint is dry, cut out the footprint and then help the child use a permanent marker to draw eyes and a mouth on it. Next, have him glue on construction paper arms, a nose, and a scarf. Display these frosty friends on a wall or bulletin board with paper snowdrifts and cutout snowflakes.

Shelley Williams—Three- and Four-Year-Olds
Children's College
Layton, UT

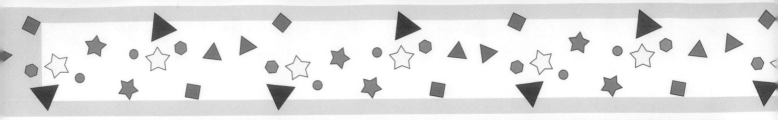

What's the catch of the day? This lovely valentine display! Provide each child with a large red heart cutout and three small pink heart cutouts. Invite the child to glue the hearts together to create a fish; then have him use glitter glue pens and markers to decorate his fish. Display youngsters' fish on a bulletin board with cutout starfish and seaweed; then add a title similar to the one shown. You won't need to fish for compliments with this idea!

Maria Rotberg—Three-Year-Olds, Prince of Peace Educational Center, Howell, NJ

Give a Western flair to a valentine display with this idea. Make a class supply of a Wanted poster similar to the one shown. Photograph each child wearing a cowboy hat; then glue the developed photo to the middle of the poster. Or use a digital camera and print each child's picture onto a poster as shown. Display the posters on a bulletin board and add the title shown.

Maria Niebruegge—Preschool Special Education, Blue Ridge Elementary, Columbia, MO

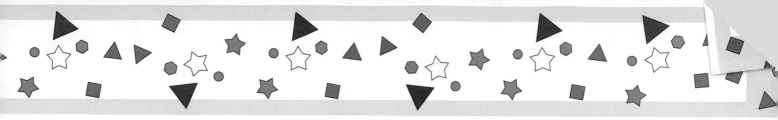

This display is sure to stir up lots of conversation about shadows and seasons! Mount a silhouette of a groundhog on a large oval cutout. Attach a speech balloon with the display's caption "When will winter end?" Around this, place silhouettes you've made of each child with his answer to the groundhog's question.

Donna Pollhammer—Three-Year-Olds
YMCA Chipmunk Preschool
Westminster, MD

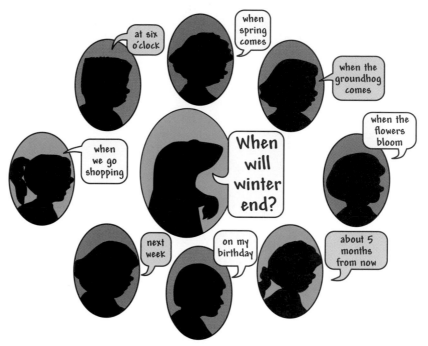

Here's a magical March display! Have children make a large handprint rainbow on a sheet of bulletin board paper. Cut out the rainbow. Staple a Poly-Fil fiber fill cloud to a bulletin board; then mount the rainbow on the board so that it is coming out of the cloud. Staple a construction paper pot of gold at the end of the rainbow. Glue each child's picture on a separate construction paper gold coin; then mount the coins around the pot.

Bonnie Martin—Preschool
Hopewell Country Day School
Pennington, NJ

This creepy-crawly attendance display provides learning opportunities for your circle time! Cut a picture of each child into a circle; then laminate the photos. Also laminate a class supply (plus one extra) of large green construction paper circles. Mount the circles on a wall near your group area to create the caterpillar, adding facial features to the first circle and the loop side of a Velcro piece to each of the other circles. Attach the hook side of a Velcro piece to the back of each photo. When a child creeps into your room, she puts her photo on a circle. Count the faces present and not present each day!

Tina Mrozek—Two-Year-Olds, Children's World, Lisle, IL

Plip, plop—here come the raindrops! Mount a storm cloud cutout above an outdoor scene. Invite your youngsters to cut raindrops from metallic paper (or aluminum foil). Staple the rain to the board. Then help each child dip his hand in brown tempera paint and make a handprint near the bottom of the board as shown. Oh, lovely mud!

Leah Treen and Chris Lewis—Four-Year-Olds, Hillwood Baptist Preschool, Huntsville, AL

Catch the eyes of passersby with this beautiful butterfly display. Have each child fill a resealable plastic bag with colorful pieces of tissue paper. Bend a pipe cleaner in half around the middle of the bag. Then twist the pipe cleaner to create the butterfly's antennae and body. Mount the butterflies on a bulletin board and then add student-made springtime scenery.

Tammy Gehrig
Windlake Elementary
Milwaukee, WI

1. You like yellow.
2. You eat pizza.
3. You help at church.
4. You drive a van.
5. You like to cook.

This guessing game will be a hit for Mother's Day! Have each child draw a picture of his mother. Then have him dictate five clues about his mom. Tape a strip of paper over each of the last four clues; then display the clues under the picture. Each day, reveal an additional clue, and encourage moms to pick out their pictures. On the last day, mount photos on the matching drawings to reveal the identities.

Anjali Gadre—PreK, Good Shepherd Christian Day Care, Somerville, NJ

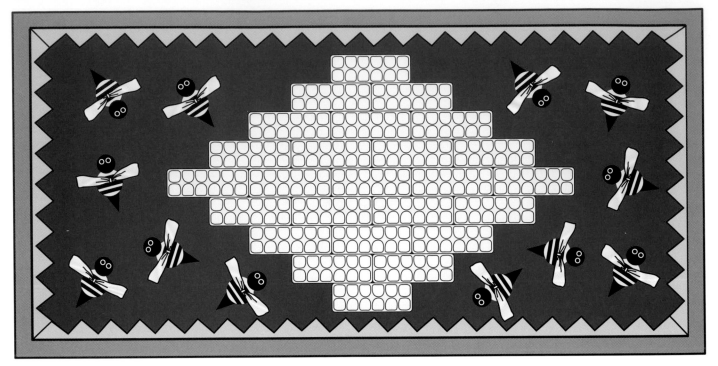

What can you make with 25 yellow egg cartons? A bulletin board beehive! Cut the bottom off of each egg carton and staple it to a bulletin board as shown. Have each child make a construction paper bee with hole reinforcers for eyes and plastic-wrap wings. Staple the bees around the hive, and this display is sure to cause quite a buzz!

Jill Glass—Preschool and Extended Kindergarten, Gaston Elementary, Gaston, IN

This tree is sure to become a favorite gathering place for group time and storytime! To create the tree's trunk and branches, cut wood-grained Con-Tact paper and then mount the pieces to the walls in a corner of your room. Depending on the season, hang large leaves, apples, or snowflakes from the ceiling directly in front of the tree. Hang the items with matching colors of yarn and vary the height at which they are displayed to create a truly inviting effect.

Angelia Dagnan—One- to Three-Year-Olds
Royale Childcare and Learning Center
Knoxville, TN

80

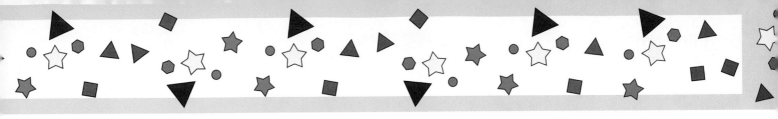

Inching Our Way Toward Kindergarten

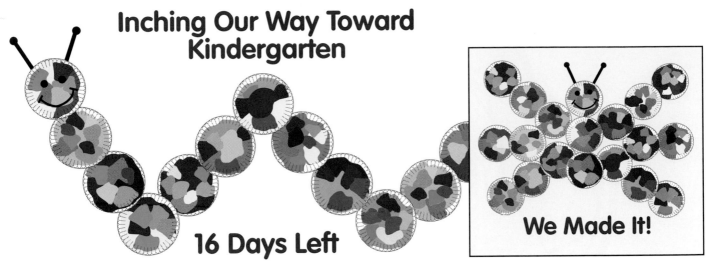

16 Days Left

We Made It!

The end-of-the-year countdown is so much more exciting with this changeable display! Have each child sponge-paint a white paper plate. Display the plates in the shape of a caterpillar; then add a title similar to the one shown. Each day, remove a different plate from the board and set it aside. Time the removal of plates so that the last caterpillar segment is removed the day before school ends. On the last day of school, reposition the plates in the shape of a butterfly and change the title to say "We Made It!"

Wendi Southwick—Three-Year-Olds, Novi Community Education Preschool, Novi, MI

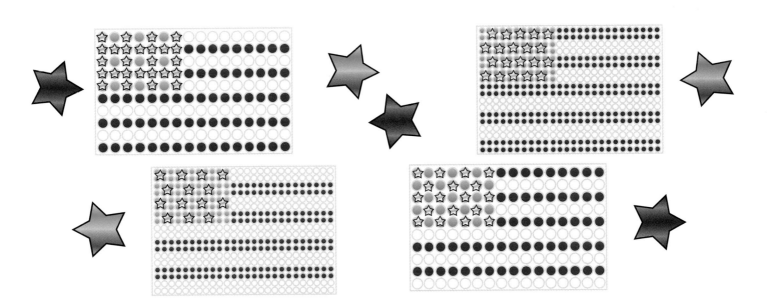

Why will this patriotic display be so "pop-ular"? The flags are made from bubble wrap! To prepare, cut a large rectangular piece of bubble wrap for each child. Next, mix a little liquid dish soap with red and blue fingerpaint (approximately 1 part soap with 3 parts fingerpaint). Have each child fingerpaint red stripes and a blue rectangle on the wrap to resemble an American flag. When the paint is dry, have the child add foil star stickers to the blue rectangle. Use loops of clear packing tape to display the flags in a window. Then add red and blue cellophane stars to complete this translucent display.

Diann Kroos—Preschool, Donald O. Clifton Child Development, Lincoln, NE

Dog Pattern

Use with the bulletin board idea
on page 72.

Write

Snowman Kit

"Apple-lutely Tree-mendous"!

Supplement your apple theme with this great craft that strengthens children's fingers. To make one apple tree, place an open brown lunch bag on a flat surface. Starting at the bottom, twist half of the bag into a trunk shape. Tear strips from the open end of the bag down to the twisted part; then twist the strips to form the branches. Glue red pom-pom apples onto the branches. It's "apple-lutely" terrific!

Elaine Holdt—Special Needs
    Preschool
Potential Development Program
Youngstown, OH

Every Piece Counts

Use this idea to help your little ones feel a sense of belonging in your classroom. Purchase one or two puzzles so that you have as many pieces as you have children in your class. (Consider purchasing a duplicate puzzle to prepare for lost or forgotten pieces.) Before the beginning of school, mail each student a puzzle piece along with a note asking her to bring the piece on the first day. When the children arrive, invite them to work together to assemble the puzzle. What a wonderful way to begin the year!

Nancy Goldberg—Three-Year-Olds
B'nai Israel Nursery School
Rockville, MD

Lace a Placemat

If you have some old vinyl placemats, use them to make durable lacing cards for your preschoolers. Cut the placemats into desired shapes and then punch holes around the edges of each shape. What a simple and inexpensive way to lace up some learning!

Jill Beattie—Four- and Five-Year-Olds
Apple Place Nursery School
Chambersburg, PA

Bake a Batch of Friendship!

Teaching cooperation and color mixing is a piece of cake with this unique idea! Use a mix to prepare white cake batter. Then fill a small cup with batter for each child. Invite each child to stir her choice of food coloring into her cup of batter; then have all the children pour their batter into a greased sheet-cake pan. After little ones have admired the cool color swirls, bake the cake according to the package directions. Once the cake has cooled, serve it with whipped topping and colored sprinkles. What a colorful and tasty treat!

Karen Sheheane—Preschool
United Methodist Preschool, Tallahassee, FL

Comfort in a Pocket

Here's an idea for comforting young ones who are having difficulty transitioning into school. Glue a copy of the poem shown onto a construction paper pocket. Then paint a wooden ice-cream spoon brown. When the paint is dry, use a permanent marker to draw bear features on the spoon. Read the poem on the pocket to your preschooler; then present him with the bear and the pocket. Now when your tot needs a little tenderness, he has a pair of listening ears at all times.

Sue Fleischmann—Preschool, Holy Cross School, Menomonee Falls, WI

In my pocket is a bear.
He quietly sleeps inside of there.
I take him out when I am sad
And tell him why I feel so bad.
When I feel better, he goes back in
And then goes back to sleep again.

Turkey Tracks

Watch your preschoolers strut their stuff in these fun-to-wear turkey shoes! To make a pair, hot-glue cork strips in the shape of turkey toes (as shown) to the bottom of an old pair of shoes. Then roll out a length of bulletin board paper and prepare a large, shallow container with a thick layer of paper towels in the bottom. Pour in some tempera paint to create a giant-size stamp pad. Have one child at a time put on the shoes and step carefully into the container. Then have her step onto the paper and walk its length. Be sure to hold the child's hand as she walks to prevent her from slipping. Look—turkey tracks!

Helen K. Dening

A Touching Experience

Encourage tactile exploration with this fingerpainting idea. Set out a variety of textured materials—such as bubble wrap, aluminum foil, cardboard, and ceramic tiles—on your art table. Tape the edges of each material to the table. Next, add fingerpaint to each material and invite youngsters to take turns fingerpainting on each one. Afterward, discuss the experience with the children. Now that's a "sense-sational" experience!

Patricia Moeser—Preschool, U. W. Preschool Lab Site , Madison, WI

Lasting Leaves

Do you enjoy using real fall leaves in your fall decorations or math and movement activities but wish they didn't fall apart and lose their color? Here's a lasting solution: laminate them! Then use them during hands-on activities or hang them from your ceiling for decoration. The best part is you can use them through the season!

Joella Poulos—Preschool, Great South Bay YMCA, Bay Shore, NY

Cereal Box Bingo

If your preschoolers have an appetite for letter recognition, they'll love to play Cereal Box Bingo! Collect a number of familiar cereal boxes; then cut off the front panels to use as gameboards. Give each player a box front and a supply of cereal pieces to use as markers. Call out letters and have little ones look for and mark them on their cereal box gameboards. Teach youngsters to yell, "Bingo!" when a cereal name is completely covered. Then everyone can snack on the playing pieces!

Susan Keller—PreK
Tiro UMC Community
    Preschool
Tiro, OH

Hairy the Pumpkin

This science project is sure to inspire lots of giggles and grins! Carve a jack-o'-lantern face on a medium-size pumpkin; then stuff crumpled newspaper inside. On top, add a layer of cotton batting or Poly-Fil filling. Spray the layer with water; then ask children to help you sprinkle grass seed (such as the type for shady lawns) onto the cotton. Spray the cotton and seeds again. Place the pumpkin in a sunny area, keeping it moist by periodically misting with water. Within a week, Mr. Hairy Pumpkin will be sprouting a new crew cut!

Jeanine Trofholz—Three-Year-Olds
St. Luke's Rainbow Preschool
Columbus, NE

Kisses and a Smile

Don't you wish you could bottle up your youngsters' sweet little smiles and kisses? Now you can with this great gift idea! In advance, purchase a class supply of pint-size canning rings and jars. Cut a photograph of each student so that it will fit snugly inside the canning ring; then glue the photo inside the ring. Fill the jar with Hershey's Kisses candies, screw on the lid, and then tie a festive ribbon around the jar. Kisses and a smile from a child! What a perfect gift!

Heather Nelson—Two- and Three-Year-Olds
Adair Care for Children
Adair, IA

Penguin Bowling

What's black and white and rolls all over? A penguin bowling pin! Add some polar excitement to your classroom and exercise gross-motor skills with a game of penguin bowling. In advance, collect ten clean Chugs drink bottles or other similarly shaped plastic milk bottles. Cut off the labels; then paint the bottles black to resemble penguins. (To help the paint adhere to the plastic bottles, mix liquid dish detergent into the paint.) Leave parts of the bottle unpainted to create a white penguin belly and white eyes. Then paint an orange beak and feet. When the paint is dry, set up the pins in an open area of your classroom. Place a foam or rubber ball near the pins and invite students to use the ball for some penguin bowling!

Mileen McGee—Pre-K
George O. Barr Elementary
Silvis, IL

Fluffy White Stuff

Here's an easy technique for adding wispy snow flurries to any artwork. To begin, rub a glue stick onto the area to be covered in snow. Then repeatedly dab a cotton ball onto the sticky area. Bits of fluffy cotton will stick to the glue. Presto—snow! If your students really enjoy doing this, have them use the same technique someday to create white fur. They'll love it!

Tina Marie Pisarski—Preschool
The Goddard School of Woodbridge, Iselin, NJ

Reindeer Noses

Here's a clever Christmas gift your pre-schoolers will love! For each child, partially fill a snack-size resealable plastic bag with red cinnamon candies. Type the poem shown, duplicate it, and staple a copy to each bag. What a neat treat!

Sarah Booth—Four- and Five-Year-Olds
Messiah Nursery School
South Williamsport, PA

I wanted the perfect gift for you,
But couldn't decide just what to do!
I almost sent you a dozen roses—
Instead here's a bag of reindeer noses!

Snowman Kit

If there's a blanket of white snow covering your town, your little ones will love this idea for getting parents involved in learning! Prepare a snowman kit for each child by filling a paper grocery bag with two lumps of charcoal (for eyes), a carrot (for a nose), a length of yarn (for a mouth), a piece of fabric (for a scarf), and two twigs (for arms). Slip in a note asking parents to help their child build a snowman and to add a hat of the child's choice from home. Also ask that they take a photo of the finished snow-man to return to school. Display all the snowman photos for everyone to enjoy!

Mary Gribble—Three- and Four-Year-Olds, Country Goose Preschool, River Falls/Prescott, WI

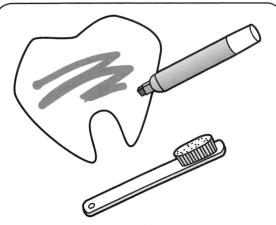

Wipe-Off Teeth

Studying dental health? Make some teeth your little ones will want to brush again and again! For each child, cut a tooth shape from white poster board. Laminate all the tooth cutouts. Give one to each student, along with a child's toothbrush and some dry-erase markers. Invite children to get their teeth "dirty" and then brush them "clean"! Discuss foods that are good and bad for teeth as your little ones work.

Kristi Ingram—Four-Year-Olds
Mother's Day Out Nursery School
Cross Lanes, WV

Containers for Your Dough

If you make your own play dough, you'll like this storage suggestion. Whenever you make a batch of dough, store it in one or more Crystal Light containers. They have tight seals and lids in several colors. If desired, match the lid and dough colors for color-coded storage.

Patti Kasprzak—Pre-K
The Kids' Castle, Barrington, NJ

Groundhog Mask

Use this song and mask to get your little ones searching for their shadows on Groundhog Day (February 2). To make one mask, cut out two eyeholes from a brown paper plate. Then have a child glue on construction paper ears, cheeks, teeth, and a nose. Tape a jumbo craft stick to the back of the mask. Teach your students the song below and then take them outside on a shadow search!

(sung to the tune of "I'm a Little Teapot")

I'm a little groundhog,
Small and round.
I sleep in a burrow
Deep in the ground.
I look to find my shadow
On Groundhog Day
To tell you if spring is
On its way!

craft idea by Sarah Booth—Pre-K
Messiah Nursery School, South Williamsport, PA

Hey, a Stamp With Me on It!

Wouldn't you love it if your children could address their own valentines? They can! Take a photo of each child (or use a wallet-size school photo of each child). Align the photos on a large sheet of paper and label each one with the child's name. Use a photocopier to reduce the page so that the photos are about the size of large stamps. If you'd like to perforate the stamps so they can be torn off the sheet like real stamps, use a sewing machine to stitch perforated lines through several pages at one time. It really works! Send a sheet of these awesome valentine stamps home with each child to make addressing valentines a breeze.

Gina Christensen—Preschool
Newton, KS

Cupcake Caves

Spring is approaching and the bears are coming out of hibernation. Invite your little ones to wake up some friendly bears from their long winter's nap with this cooking project. Have students help you prepare a boxed cake mix according to the package directions for making cupcakes. But before baking, push a Teddy Grahams snack into each cup of batter. Then bake and cool as directed. Frost the cupcake caves and pass them out to your youngsters. They'll love finding the bears inside! Wake up, bears!

Carol Breeding—Preschool, New Life Center Daycare, Des Moines, IA

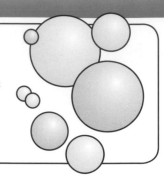

Colored Bubble Art

Add a twist to your bubble fun this summer with a hint of color! Simply mix a little liquid watercolor or food coloring into your favorite bubble solution. Set out white paper; then invite youngsters to blow bubbles toward the paper. As the bubbles hit the paper and pop, they'll leave behind a colorful impression!

Kristen Miller—Two- and Three-Year-Olds, Early Childhood Development Center, Notre Dame, IN

Easy Easter Egg Treats

Revive your favorite crispy rice treats recipe to make these flavorful Easter eggs. To prepare the mixture, microwave one-quarter cup of butter and ten ounces of marshmallows for two minutes. Quickly mix in three ounces of any flavor of Jell-O gelatin. Then stir in six cups of crispy rice cereal. Apply nonstick cooking spray to each child's clean hands. Give each child a large spoonful of the warm mixture to form into an egg shape. Cover each egg with colorful plastic wrap and then tie the wrap with a ribbon. New and improved treats!

Colleen Keller—Preschool and
Pre-K
Clarion-Goldfield Elementary
Clarion, IA

Color-Changing Cubes

Want to serve your little ones some lemonade on a hot summer day? Don't pass up the opportunity to turn it into a color-mixing lesson! To prepare, tint the water in a few ice cube trays with blue or red food coloring; then freeze the cubes. When you prepare the lemonade, add a squirt of yellow food coloring to enhance the color. Then pour a cup for each child and invite him to drop in a colored ice cube or two. Stir it up and…cool!

Donna Leonard—Head Start
Dyersville Head Start
Dyersville, IA

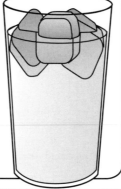

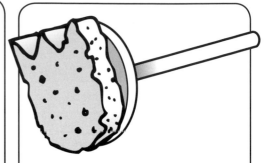

Push-Ups for Painting

After your class enjoys a treat of frozen push-up pops, save the round plastic bases with the long handles attached. They're great for sponge painting! Just hot-glue a sponge shape to the round disc. The handle makes printing the sponge shape easy for little hands!

Vicki Lehr—
    Four- and Five-Year-Olds
Bethel Nursery School
Indianapolis, IN

Playground Pipe

Here's a new angle on playground fun—a PVC pipe roll! To make one, attach a six- to eight-foot length of PVC pipe to a fence on your playground. Attach the pipe at a slight angle, not too far off the ground. Then provide tennis balls and small toy cars for youngsters to roll through the pipe.

Cathy Consford—Director, Buda Primary Early Learning Center, Buda, TX

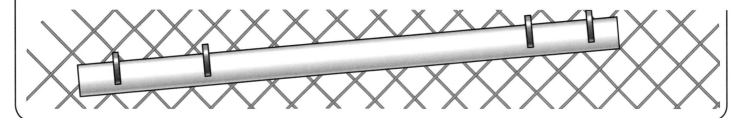

Theme Units

Preschoolers, Start Your Engines!

Zoom into a new year of preschool with the car-themed ideas in this welcome unit. Your new students will soon find out that preschool is "wheel-y" fun!

by Ada Goren

Dear Parent,

Preschool License

Full name:
Jackson Crane
Birthdate:
June 19, 2000
Likes to be called:
Jackson
Some favorite things:
spaghetti, soccer
Wants to learn:
to tie my shoes

May I See Your License, Please?

Steer your students into preschool with a welcome note that has a "race-y" flair! Make one copy of the open page (page 94) and use it to write a note to your students, introducing yourself and telling them about the upcoming school year. In the note, explain that you'd like each student and her parents to fill out the blank preschool license included with your letter. Then photocopy both your note and the license on page 95 to make a class supply. Tuck a copy of your note and a blank license into an envelope for each child. For fun, include a photo of you in your car.

On the first day of school, collect each child's license. Then bind all the licenses between construction paper covers to create a class book. Title the book "We're Licensed to Learn! Meet the Preschool Drivers in [your name]'s Class." Flip through your license log during a group time and share the information about each child. Then give each youngster an opportunity to take the book home for a night so his family can get to know his classmates, too.

Cubby Tags

These license plate look-alikes will add to the auto atmosphere and help youngsters identify their cubbies. For each child, program a 5" x 8" unlined index card with your school and class names as shown. Use alphabet stickers to spell out the child's name across the center of the card. Adhere each child's license plate cubby tag to her cubby with clear Con-Tact paper. Now your little drivers will know just where to park their belongings!

Sunny Days Preschool

DANIELLE

Mrs. Kane's Threes

Preschool Parking Lot

Beep! Beep! Make way for these simple nametags that can also be used on an attendance and helper display! Make a class supply of the car patterns on page 96 on various colors of construction paper. Program each car with a different child's name; then laminate the cars and cut them out. Punch a hole, as indicated, and attach the tag to a child's clothing with a safety pin.

To create an attendance chart and helper display all in one, first cover a bulletin board with black paper. Use yellow masking tape to create as many parking spaces as you have children in your class. To create a few reserved parking spaces along the bottom of the board, use a white crayon or paint pen to print the names of your classroom helpers. Place a bit of Sticky-Tac on each parking space to hold the laminated car patterns in place. Park a car in each space, designating which children will be helpers by parking their cars in the reserved spaces. When a youngster arrives at school, remove her car from the display and pin it to her clothing. You'll be able to see at a glance who's left in the lot—or in other words, who's here and who's not!

On the Road Again

These tips will "auto-matically" make your annual school tour more fun! To prepare for your tour, create lines with yellow chalk (on outdoor pavement and sidewalks) and/or yellow masking tape (on indoor floors and carpets) to make your route resemble a street. Photocopy the stop sign on page 96 on red construction paper, making one sign for each area of the school you wish to have little ones visit. Cut out the stop signs and post one at each of your intended stops. On the day of your tour, give each child a paper plate steering wheel and invite your class to travel in a car caravan as you lead the tour. Let's drive!

Rules of the Road

To keep your students safe, avoid traffic jams, and make things run smoothly in your classroom, you'll need to introduce your new preschoolers to a few rules. To prepare, cut geometric shapes—such as triangles, rectangles, and octagons—from construction paper. Draw a black outline around each one so that it resembles a traffic sign. Then discuss class rules during a group time. Write each rule on a separate traffic sign and add a simple drawing. Post the signs in your classroom and your youngsters will soon be cruising along with good behavior!

Pam Crane

Get Your Keys and Go

What are the keys to making a smooth transition? For this idea, they're your car keys! When you want youngsters to move from one activity to the next, pull out your car keys and give them a shake to get youngsters' attention. Then recite the chant below—inserting your next activity in the last line—to get your preschoolers to shift gears.

Now it's time to turn the key.
Start your car and drive with me!
Where to next? Do you know?
It's time to [wash our hands]. Let's go!

Honk If You Love Preschool!

Your little ones will love providing the sound effects for this simple song, which helps with learning classmates' names. During a group time, teach youngsters the song below and demonstrate how to squeeze a bicycle horn in rhythm for the last two lines. Give the horn to a child and sing the song, inserting the child's name in the first line. Invite him to honk the horn in rhythm at the end of the verse. If you can't find a bicycle horn, instead give each child her steering wheel from "On the Road Again" (page 91) and have her say "Honk, honk, honk!" as she presses the center of her steering wheel. Keep going until you've sung to each of your students and everyone has had a chance to toot to the tune!

(sung to the tune of "Where Is Thumbkin?")

Hello, [child's name].
Hello, [child's name].
How are you? How are you?
Honk if you love preschool!
Honk if you love preschool!
(Honk, honk, honk!)
(Honk, honk, honk!)

Heading for the Drive-Thru

Where do preschool motorists stop for a snack? At the drive-thru, of course! Decorate the outside of a puppet theater to resemble a fast-food drive-up window. Or cut off the top, the bottom, and one side of a large appliance box; then cut a window in the remaining center section. Paint the box and decorate it to resemble a drive-up window. Little ones can take turns role-playing the server inside the restaurant, passing individually bagged snacks to each preschool driver who rolls by at snacktime. During center time, encourage youngsters to use the drive-thru in your dramatic-play area. Or take the drive-thru outside for some speedy outdoor play. No telling what will be on the menu at this restaurant!

Heigh-Ho, the Stoplight-O

Accelerate the fun with this movement activity that also encourages little ones to follow directions. In advance, prepare a paper stoplight by gluing a red, a yellow, and a green circle onto a black rectangle. Show youngsters the stoplight and review the meaning of each color. Then give youngsters the steering wheels prepared for "On the Road Again" (page 91). Explain that they may drive all around your classroom but that they must obey the lights. Then teach youngsters this song. As you sing each verse, point to the appropriate color on the stoplight. Have your youngsters "drive" around the room, following the directions of the stoplight and the song. Repeat the tune until your little motorists run out of gas.

Jacob
(child's name)

is
rolling right along
in preschool!

Ms. Pegram   8/25/04
(teacher's signature)   (date)

Rolling Right Along

If painting with toy cars is an art activity you never tire of, invite youngsters to decorate these "wheel-y" cute awards! For each child, photocopy the award on page 97 on construction paper; then fill it out. In your art area, set out a few paper plates of tempera paint in different colors. Gather at least one toy car or truck for each paint color. Invite a child to roll a vehicle through a paint color and then "drive" the car across the edges of her award to make tracks. Encourage her to repeat the process with another color of paint if she likes, keeping the painted tracks around the edges of the award. Set the papers aside to dry; then send the awards home to show how very proud you are of your new preschoolers!

(sung to the tune of
"The Farmer in the Dell")

Green means go!
Green means go!
Heigh-ho, the stoplight-o,
Green means go!

Yellow means slow down.
Yellow means slow down.
Heigh-ho, the stoplight-o,
Yellow means slow down.

Red means stop.
Red means stop.
Heigh-ho, the stoplight-o,
Red means stop.

93

Open Page

Use with "May I See Your License, Please?" on page 90.

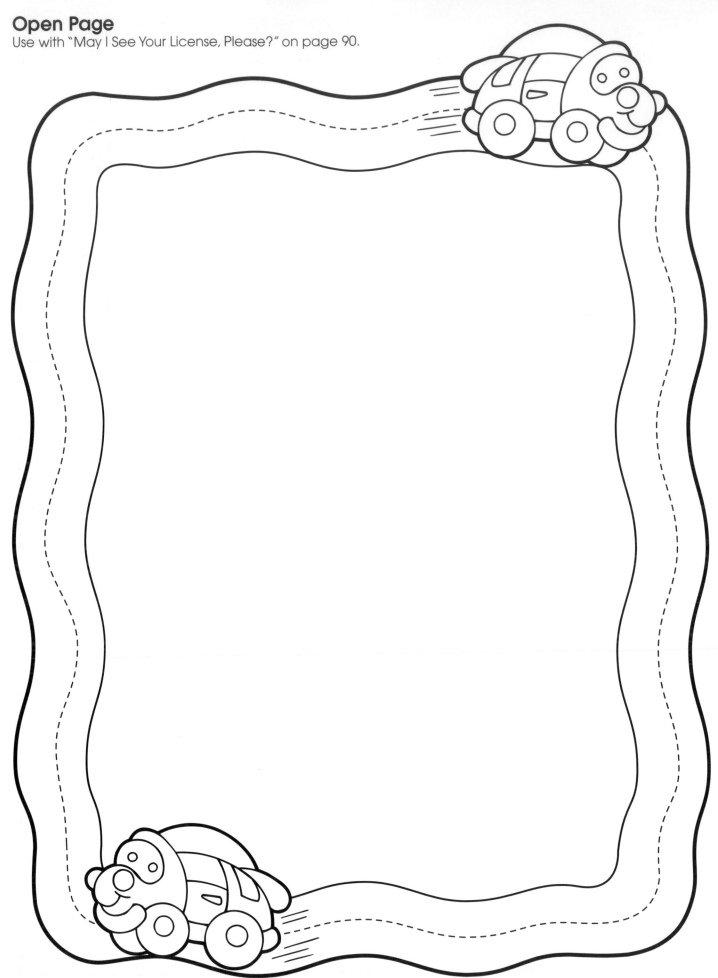

Preschool License

Full name: _____

Birthdate: _____

Likes to be called: _____

Attach
photo
here.

Some favorite things: _____

Wants to learn: _____

Car Patterns
Use with "Preschool Parking Lot" on page 91.

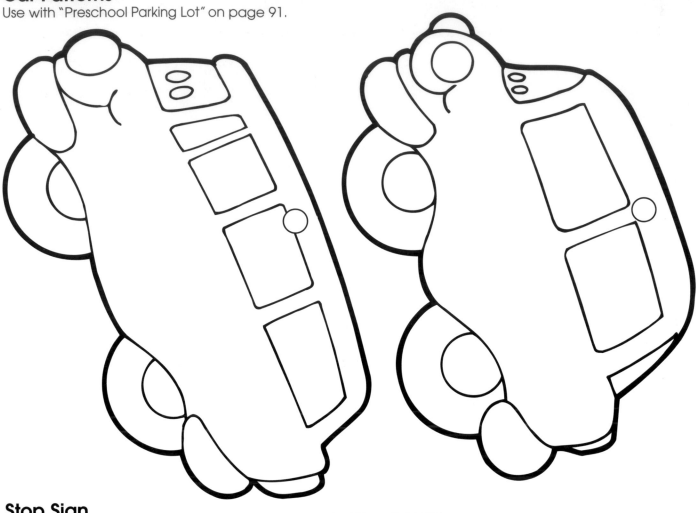

Stop Sign
Use with "On the Road Again"
on page 91.

STOP

©The Education Center, Inc. • *The Best of* The Mailbox® • *Preschool* • TEC60784

(child's name)

is

rolling right along
in preschool!

(teacher's signature)

(date)

Fishing for Names

We have a net full of ideas to help the little fish in your school learn all about names! You'll find ideas that celebrate each child's name, followed by ideas that help younger preschoolers learn to recognize their names and their friends' names in print. If you have older preschoolers, or if you are using this collection later in the school year, you'll want to reel in the ideas that focus on identifying, matching, sequencing, and forming the individual letters in names. You name it, it's here!

Group Time, Home-School Connection

Name Acclaim

Your claim to fame is your name! Even if you're not famous, people *do* know you by name. So celebrate names with this class book. Send a note home asking each parent to briefly explain how her child got his name or what his name means. To ensure that every child has a page, use a baby names book to find the meaning of every child's name. Type or write each explanation on a colorful piece of paper; then add the child's picture. Don't forget to make a page explaining your own name. Laminate the pages, if desired, before binding them together in alphabetical order. Share the book with the class often or send it home for families to enjoy.

Dayle Timmons—Special Education-Inclusion
Alimacani Elementary School
Jacksonville, FL

Rebekah
Rebekah means "enchantingly beautiful."
It was Rebekah's grandma's name.

Discovery Center

The Bigger the Name, the Better!

A magnifying lens and these personalized picture cards are all you'll need to get youngsters excited about name recognition. To prepare this center, glue each child's photo (or a color copy) onto a separate piece of tagboard and then write his name on it. Put the pictured cards in the center along with magnifying lenses. Then encourage youngsters to take a closer look!

Tarika

Leah, James, Zack...Goose!

No one will duck out of group time when you play this fun game that helps children learn the names of their new classmates! Seat children in a circle in an open area. Ask one child to volunteer to walk around the circle. As she taps each child on the head, the whole class says that child's name, and then the volunteer repeats the child's name. When desired, the volunteer chooses to say "goose" instead of repeating the child's name. The volunteer, chased by that child, then runs around the circle and sits back in that child's spot. The new child takes his turn tapping.

Kathy Houser, R. C. Lindsey School, Chesterland, OH

Name TV

Now here's some high-quality programming—provided by our viewers! To make a simple video that will help students learn each other's names, provide each child with a large piece of paper with his name written on it. Briefly film each child holding his name and introducing himself. If desired, ask each child a question. Show the video during quiet snacktimes or at open house. It's a hit!

Dawn Michelle Schu—Preschool
Resurrection Preschool
Chicago, IL

Photographic Memory

Youngsters will enjoy concentrating on this game, which features their classmates' pictures and names. To make the game, take a close-up picture of each child; then have duplicates developed. Cut as many cardboard squares as you have photos, or recycle the squares from a traditional Concentration game from which pieces are missing. Cut each photo to the size of a square, glue it onto the square, and then cover the photo with cold laminating film for durability. Write students' names on the squares. To play, a child turns all squares photo sides down and then plays as he would Concentration until he matches all pairs. As a child plays, point out the names written on the squares and the letter that each name starts with.

Kathy Hurford—Four- and Five-Year-Olds
Tri-Cap Head Start
Boonville, IN

S.S. Moniker

Art Center

What's the Magic Name?

This fun painting center will show children the magic of a good name. To prepare, use a white candle or white crayon to write each child's name on a separate piece of painting paper. (On the back of each piece, write the child's name in small print so you can quickly match the magic name with the correct child.) When a child visits the painting center, direct him to use thinned tempera paint or watercolors to paint his paper. Hey! That's my name!

Dayle Timmons—Special Education-Inclusion
Alimacani Elementary School
Jacksonville, FL

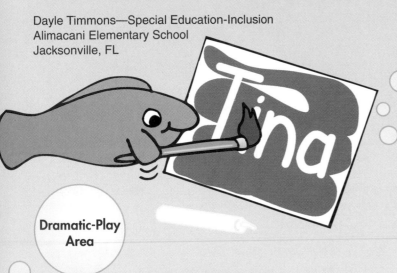

Movement

Swirling, Twirling Names

So simple. So easy. So fun! Use a dark marker to write each child's name on a length of crepe paper streamer. During a group time invite each child to move her streamer and watch her name in motion as you play various styles of music.

Discovery Center

Name in a Bottle

Chances are you've filled plastic bottles with water and colorful items such as confetti for youngsters to enjoy in your discovery center. Here's a twist on that idea that improves name recognition! Prepare one or more of the bottles by filling them with water and plastic confetti pieces. Then use a permanent marker to write each child's name on a separate piece of clear plastic, such as a small rectangle cut from a plastic lid or empty plastic container. Put one or two names in each bottle you've prepared. Then, each day, replace the names with new names. Whose name is spinning in the bottle today?

Dramatic-Play Area

Funny Money

Any time you invest in making this money is sure to earn big returns with your little ones! To make some toy money that features your students' faces and names, make at least a class supply of the money pattern on page 103 on green paper. Cut a close-up photo of each child to the size of the oval in the center of the money. Glue each photo to a separate bill; then write the child's name on the bill. Laminate the money for durability; then cut it out. Place the money in a dramatic-play area such as a housekeeping area or a grocery store. How much money do you have? I have a Kelly and an Aaron…and they're worth a lot!

Water Table

Wetter Letters

Teaching youngsters the letters in their names can be wet and wild fun when you add die-cut craft foam letters to your water table! Determine the number of each different letter you need to spell any child's name. Die-cut that amount of each letter from craft foam; then put the letters in the water table. Help a child find the letters that spell his name; then encourage him to stick the wet letters to a side of the water table.

Dayle Timmons—Special Education-Inclusion
Alimacani Elementary School
Jacksonville, FL

Group Time

The Name of the Game

Help youngsters focus on the letters that spell their names with this group activity. To prepare, determine the number of each different letter you need to spell any child's name. Use a black marker to program large paper plates with capital letters so that you have the correct letters in the correct amounts. Also use a black marker to write each child's name in capital letters on a separate card. During a group time, show a name card. Ask a group of children to help you find the letters that spell the child's name on the card. Then have a different child hold each letter. Sing the following song to ask the child whose name is being spelled to help you put the children in the correct order.

As a variation, program the uppercase letters needed in black on large paper plates. Program the lowercase letters needed in red on smaller paper plates. Similarly program name cards. Happy spelling!

*(sung to the tune of
"He's Got the Whole World in His Hands")*

We've got all the letters for [Christy's] name.
We've got all the letters for [Christy's] name.
We've got all the letters for [Christy's] name.
[Christy], help us spell your name!

Dayle Timmons

Fine-Motor Center

Letter Clip

If you made the name cards for "The Name of the Game," use them again along with clothespins for this fine-motor activity. If desired, attach each child's photo to his name card. Program clothespins with uppercase letters only (black marker) or uppercase and lowercase letters (black marker and red marker) so that you have enough of each letter to spell each child's name. Encourage a child to clip matching clothespins onto his name card to spell his name.

Dayle Timmons

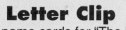

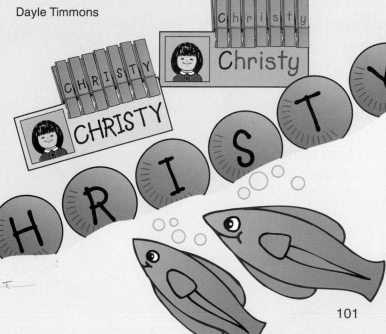

Games Center

Puzzling Names

Youngsters will scramble to the games center to use their problem-solving skills on these name puzzles. To make a puzzle for each child, use a colored marker to write each letter of his name on a separate craft stick. Use the same marker to write the child's name on a list of class names. Write the different children's names using as many colors of markers as possible. When a child visits the center, he chooses a name from the list and then finds all of the sticks with letters written in that color. To spell the name, he looks at the list, selects the correct sticks, and then arranges them in order.

Dayle Timmons—Special Education-Inclusion
Alimacani Elementary School
Jacksonville, FL

Painting Area

Artistic Letters

Invite youngsters to practice letter formation at the painting center. Write each child's name in large letters on several sheets of painting paper. Invite each child to paint over the letters of his name. My name starts with a big, red *D!*

Home-School Connection

Claim It With Your Name!

Congratulate each child for learning how to recognize, spell, or write her name by giving her name labels to take home. Use a computer to print about five name labels for each child. Carefully cut the labels apart; then ask each child to use markers to decorate them. To prepare an envelope for each child to take her labels home in, duplicate the envelope pattern on page 103. Fill in the information on the envelope. Cut it out, fold it, and then tape the two side flaps and bottom flap together as shown. Slip each child's labels in her envelope, fold down the top flap, and send the envelope home. Hurray! Your students know about their names!

Art Center

Slippery Writing

To help each child learn to form the letters in his name, pull out the fingerpaint! Use a permanent marker to write each child's name on a piece of vinyl placemat. Encourage each child to fingerpaint over the letters in his name. Cleanup only takes a swipe with a wet sponge! Ready to try again?

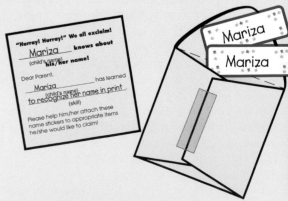

Envelope Pattern
Use with "Claim It With Your Name!" on page 102.

"Hurray! Hurray!" We all exclaim!

_____ **knows about**
child's name
his/her name!

Dear Parent,

_____ has learned
(child's name)

_____.
(skill)

Please help him/her attach these name stickers to appropriate items he/she would like to claim!

©The Education Center, Inc.

Pumpkin Science

Pokin' around the pumpkin patch we found lots of activities to develop youngsters' science process skills. It's time for your preschool scientists to ponder the properties of pumpkins. Let the investigations begin!

by Lucia Kemp Henry

Inferring

Undercover Pumpkin

Challenge your little ones to think like scientists with this guessing game. While students are out of the room, drape a cloth over a pumpkin so that it covers the pumpkin but still shows its size and shape. During a group time, use the riddle in the speech bubble to prompt the class to guess the identity of the hidden pumpkin. Your curious kiddies will become science sleuths quicker than you can say "jack-o'-lantern!"

> Here is something you can't see. Listen to these clues to guess what it might be.
> It grows from a seed, but it isn't a weed.
> It has a stem. It sits on the ground. Its shape is kind of round.
> Its color is orange like a tangerine. It smiles at you on Halloween.

Observing

huge

bumpy

yellow orange

Pumpkin Perceptions

Once your students have identified the seasonal subject to be studied, lead them in using their observation skills to learn more about the pumpkin. Have your group sit in a circle on the floor around the pumpkin. In turn, invite pairs of children to sit by the pumpkin so that they can touch it, smell it, and look at it closely. Encourage the children to communicate their observations by sharing words that describe the size, shape, color, and texture of the pumpkin. Record the words used to describe the pumpkin on separate cards. Later, reinforce these new science words by using them in the peppy, pumpkin-themed song that follows on page 105.

Descriptive Ditty

Your students will be pros at describing pumpkins after singing this descriptive ditty. Add new verses to the song by replacing the bold words with the words you recorded on cards in "Pumpkin Perceptions" on page 104. Singing is a great way to communicate scientific findings!

(sung to the tune of "Pawpaw Patch")

Where, oh, where can we find pumpkins?
Where, oh, where can we find pumpkins?
Where can we find **round, round** pumpkins?
Way down yonder in the pumpkin patch!

Where, oh, where can we find pumpkins?
Where, oh, where can we find pumpkins?
Where can we find **bumpy** pumpkins?
Way down yonder in the pumpkin patch!

Making Models

Model Pumpkins

It's natural for preschool science studies to include model making, especially when models are molded from play dough! To prepare, use your favorite recipe to make a large batch of orange play dough. If desired, also prepare a batch of brown play dough for students to use to make stems. Invite each child to a center to feel the entire surface of the same pumpkin that was used for the previous activities. Then give the child a portion of the dough to shape into a miniature model of the pumpkin. Display the real pumpkin, the pumpkin models, and the word cards together on a table. Now that's a model way for your little ones to record their pumpkin observations!

Pam Crane

A Bunch of Pumpkins

Stimulate your little scientists' classification skills by having them study the features of a number of pumpkins in a variety of shapes, sizes, and colors. Have youngsters join you on the floor to take a close look at the pumpkins. Then ask them to help you divide them into several smaller groups so that the pumpkins in each group are similar. For example, group the pumpkins with brown bumps together. Or group pumpkins with and without stems. Record the descriptive phrase for each set on a separate index card. During a different group time, select one of the cards. Then challenge the students to classify the group of pumpkins by selecting the corresponding pumpkins on their own.

smooth

bumpy

Predicting

Roll, Pumpkins, Roll!

Keep on rolling with science-process skills with this activity, which gets youngsters predicting. Arrange the pumpkins from "A Bunch of Pumpkins" in a line on an uncarpeted floor. To begin, roll a ball on the floor, pointing out that you were able to roll it in a straight line. Next, pick out the roundest pumpkin in the bunch and ask students to suggest how the pumpkin is similar to the ball. Ask them to predict whether the pumpkin will roll in a straight line like the ball. Have a volunteer roll the pumpkin; then discuss the results. Have students predict and then test how well each remaining pumpkin rolls. Once youngsters have identified the best rollers, discuss why some pumpkins can stick to the straight and narrow, and why some pumpkins can't!

The Inside Scoop

Now that students have examined the outsides of pumpkins, it's time to explore what's inside a pumpkin! To prepare, cover a table with newspaper or a vinyl tablecloth; then set a large pumpkin on the table. Invite students to describe the outside of the pumpkin; then ask each child to share what he thinks the *inside* of the pumpkin is like. Next, cut the top off the pumpkin so that students can inspect the inside and make some discoveries. Prompt hands-on observations by asking some questions:

What does the inside of the pumpkin look like?
What does it smell like?
What does it feel like?
How is the inside different from the outside of the pumpkin?

Invite each child, in turn, to help spoon out the seeds and the inside of the pumpkin. Save the rest of the pumpkin to use in "Pumpkin Squish Test" to the right.

Pumpkin Squish Test

Use this discovery center activity to squeeze some more science out of the humble pumpkin! To prepare, cut the pumpkin shell from "The Inside Scoop" into chunks. Simmer half of the chunks until the pulp is soft. Put the cooked and uncooked chunks in an empty sensory tub. Invite youngsters to discover which chunks of pumpkin are squishable and which ones aren't! Then help them describe how the chunks look and feel different.

How Does a Pumpkin Grow?

Your science-focused pumpkin study wouldn't be complete without reading one of these books about how pumpkins grow. Share and discuss *Pumpkin Pumpkin* by Jeanne Titherington or *The Pumpkin Patch* by Elizabeth King. Then wrap up your unit with a song to help your little ones communicate what they've learned.

(sung to the tune of "How Much Is That Doggie in the Window?")

Oh, how does a pumpkin in the patch grow? It starts with a wee tiny seed.
You plant the seed in some really good soil. Yes, that's what the pumpkin will need.

Oh, how does a pumpkin in the patch grow? It starts with a wee tiny seed.
Then you need to give the seed some water. Yes, that's what the pumpkin will need.

Oh, how does a pumpkin in the patch grow? It starts with a wee tiny seed.
The seed will need a lot of sunshine. Yes, that's what the pumpkin will need.

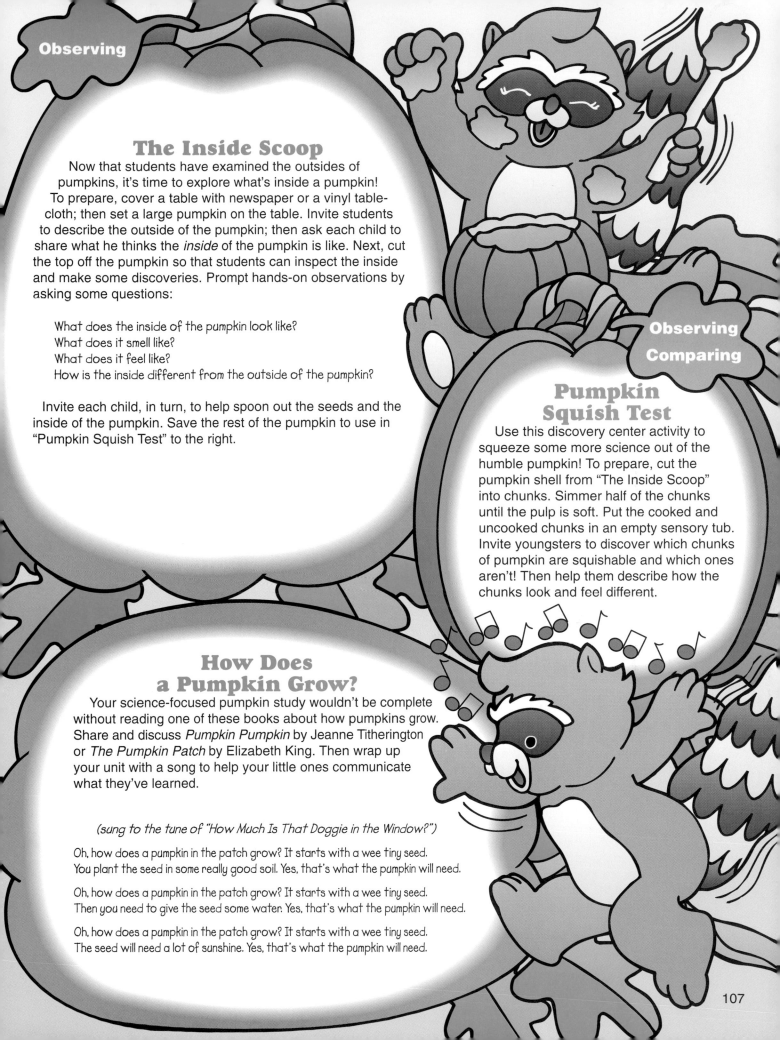

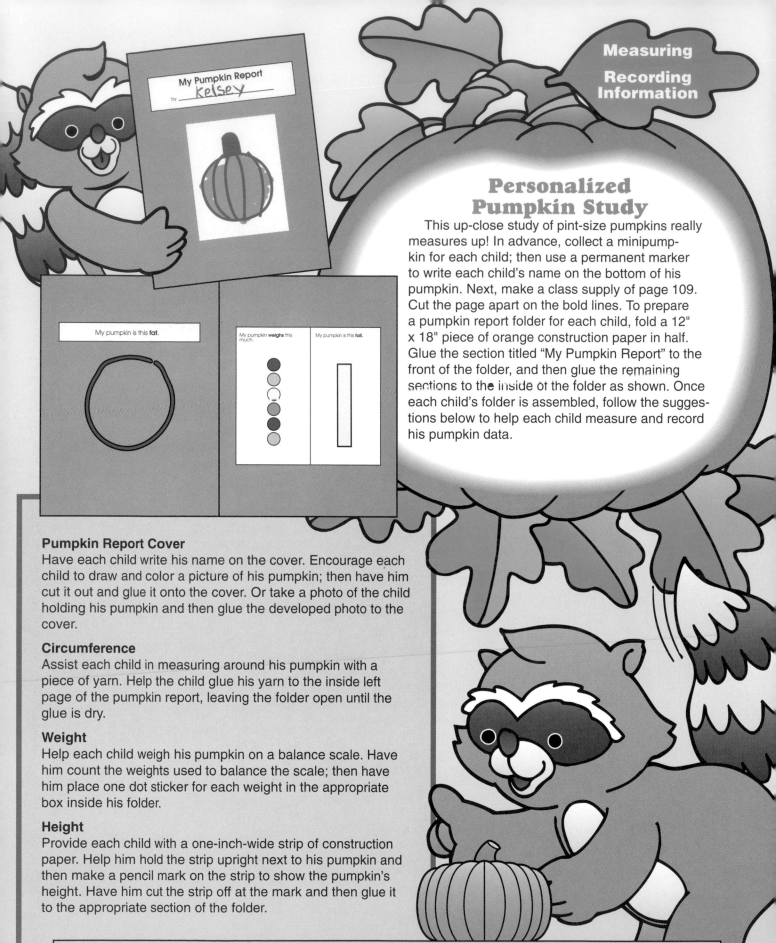

My Pumpkin Report
by Kelsey

My pumpkin is this **fat**.

My pumpkin **weighs** this much.

My pumpkin is this **tall**.

Personalized Pumpkin Study

This up-close study of pint-size pumpkins really measures up! In advance, collect a minipumpkin for each child; then use a permanent marker to write each child's name on the bottom of his pumpkin. Next, make a class supply of page 109. Cut the page apart on the bold lines. To prepare a pumpkin report folder for each child, fold a 12" x 18" piece of orange construction paper in half. Glue the section titled "My Pumpkin Report" to the front of the folder, and then glue the remaining sections to the inside of the folder as shown. Once each child's folder is assembled, follow the suggestions below to help each child measure and record his pumpkin data.

Pumpkin Report Cover
Have each child write his name on the cover. Encourage each child to draw and color a picture of his pumpkin; then have him cut it out and glue it onto the cover. Or take a photo of the child holding his pumpkin and then glue the developed photo to the cover.

Circumference
Assist each child in measuring around his pumpkin with a piece of yarn. Help the child glue his yarn to the inside left page of the pumpkin report, leaving the folder open until the glue is dry.

Weight
Help each child weigh his pumpkin on a balance scale. Have him count the weights used to balance the scale; then have him place one dot sticker for each weight in the appropriate box inside his folder.

Height
Provide each child with a one-inch-wide strip of construction paper. Help him hold the strip upright next to his pumpkin and then make a pencil mark on the strip to show the pumpkin's height. Have him cut the strip off at the mark and then glue it to the appropriate section of the folder.

My Pumpkin Report

by _____

My pumpkin is this **fat**.

My pumpkin **weighs** this much.	My pumpkin is this **tall**.

This is my family.
Let's count and see
How many people there are
And who they could be!

brother Kyle   Daddy   Mommy   Me

My Family and Me!

What are your youngsters' family ties? Find out with activities that explore the makings of a family!

ideas contributed by Mary Lou Rodriguez, Redwood City, CA

Family Fingerplay

Have youngsters follow your lead as you perform this family fingerplay; then guide students in a discussion about the different members in their families. Afterward, program a sheet of paper similar to the one shown above and then photocopy it for each child. Have the child draw a picture of her family and herself on the paper; then invite her to dictate the name and relation of each member.

This is a family.   *Show all ten fingers.*
Let's count and see
How many people there are
And who they could be!

This is the mother,   *Wiggle index finger.*
And this is the father.   *Wiggle middle finger.*
This is the sister,   *Wiggle ring finger.*
And this is the brother.   *Wiggle pinkie.*
Here is a grandpa   *Wiggle thumb.*
And a grandma too!   *Wiggle other thumb.*
An aunt,   *Wiggle other index finger.*
An uncle,   *Wiggle other middle finger.*
And cousins who   *Wiggle other ring finger*
                                        and pinkie.

The Martin Family

This is my mom, Judy. She likes to read.

This is my grandpa. I don't know his name. It's just Grandpa.

This is me, Aaron. I like to play with my cat, Buster.

This is my cat, Buster. He likes to rip things up.

Family Trees

Find out a little more about each child's family with this activity. To prepare, count the number of family members on each child's drawing from "Family Fingerplay." Then provide the child with that many leaf cutouts. (Be sure the cutouts are large enough for the child to draw on.) Invite the child to draw each family member and himself on a separate leaf. Then have the child glue each leaf onto a large construction paper tree cutout. Encourage the child to dictate a sentence or two describing each family member. Write his response near the leaf; then label the top of the tree with the child's family name. Display each child's creation in your classroom and you'll have a forest of informative family trees!

Create a Coat of Arms

In medieval times, coats of arms were used by knights as a means of identification. Today, a coat of arms is a family design and a symbol of heritage. Invite your youngsters and their families to have a little fun creating their own coats of arms. To prepare, make a tagboard shield cutout for each child's family. Divide each shield into four sections as shown. Next, photocopy the parent note on page 113 for each child. Send home a shield and note inviting each child's family to create a coat of arms. As each child returns her coat of arms, invite her to show it to the class and discuss the different symbols on it.

Campbells!

We are the Campbells!

Ya Ha Ha Ha! Ya Ha Ha Ha!

Family Actions

Does Daddy have a distinctive laugh? Does Mommy have a memorable mannerism? Invite your students to brainstorm the endearing qualities of different family members. Incorporate their responses into the song shown and then, if possible, have youngsters act it out!

(sung to the tune of "The Wheels on the Bus")

The **fathers** in the house go [student response],
[Student response], [student response].
The **fathers** in the house go [student response],
All around the house!

Sing additional verses, replacing the boldfaced word, in turn, with other family-member words, such as *mothers, sisters, brothers,*

Around-the-House Objects

Car keys, a pacifier, a tube of lipstick… Sometimes different members of families use different things and sometimes they don't! Use this engaging activity to help youngsters explore this concept. In advance, collect a variety of common objects, such as a set of car keys, a toothbrush, a tube of lipstick, a cleaning glove, a cooking utensil, and a pacifier. Place the objects in a large paper bag and invite a small group of students to join you at a center. Pull out each item, in turn, and have each child tell you which of her family members uses it. Use the objects to prompt discussions about each child's family and the roles of different members.

My mom cooks with this.

My baby brother has one of these.

111

Dinnertime!

For many families, meals are a way to spend quality time together. Invite your preschoolers to have a mock family meal with this lively adaptation of "The Farmer in the Dell." Set up a small table and chairs in your circle-time area. Lead students in a discussion about meal times with their families. Then choose one child to be the mother (or other family member, depending on the needs of your students). Have the child stand at the table as you sing the song shown. Then direct her to choose another family member to join her at the table. When all of the chairs have been filled, sing the final verse and invite the family to have a seat!

(sung to the tune of "The Farmer in the Dell")

Dinnertime is here!
Dinnertime is here!
Heigh-ho! It's time to eat.
Dinnertime is here!

The [mother] calls the [father].
The [mother] calls the [father].
Heigh-ho! It's time to eat.
The [mother] calls the [father].

Sing additional verses, replacing the underlined words with other family-member words, such as brother, granny, and grandpa.

The family all sits down.
The family all sits down.
Heigh-ho! It's time to eat!
The family all sits down.

A Family Toast!

What's the best way to wrap up your family studies? Have a family toast! Use a house-shaped cookie cutter to cut a slice of bread for each child. Toast the bread; then have the child spread peanut butter on it. (For students with peanut allergies, use soy nut butter.) Have each child count the number of people in her immediate family. Then provide her with that many teddy bear–shaped graham crackers. Direct the child to place the crackers on the house and then eat!

Scavenger Hunt Show-and-Tell

Here's a fun way to get families involved in your family unit! Have a family scavenger hunt; then have each of your preschoolers show off his family finds! To prepare, photocopy the parent note on page 113 for each child. Then staple each note to a brown paper grocery bag. As each child brings his items from home, invite him to show them to the class and talk about each treasure.

Dear Family,
　　We are learning all about families and would like your help in creating a family design on a coat of arms! Please read through the following directions. Have your family work together to create a coat of arms; then send the completed project to school with your child. Thank you for your help!

1. Write your family name in the top section.
2. Draw a family portrait in another section.
3. Draw or glue a picture of a favorite family food.
4. Draw or glue a picture of a favorite family pastime.

©The Education Center, Inc. • *The Best of* The Mailbox® • *Preschool* • TEC60784

Dear Family,
　　We would like to invite you to join our family scavenger hunt! Below you will find a list of categories. Help your child find an inexpensive item from each category that he or she can bring to school. Place the items in this bag. Your child will show the items to the class and then bring them home. Have fun searching!

• a baby item from a family member
• a hat from a family member
• junk mail with your family name on it
• a shoe from a family member
• a family photo

©The Education Center, Inc. • *The Best of* The Mailbox® • *Preschool* • TEC60784

Weather Wise

"Who-ooo" knows about the weather? Your little ones will after you share the fun ideas and activities in this unit!

by Ada Goren

Group Time

Weather Wear

Begin your weather unit with a sorting activity that will get your students thinking about what they wear in different types of weather. To prepare, label three boxes as shown. Gather a variety of children's clothing and accessories appropriate for the three types of weather.

Set up the three boxes in your group area. Show youngsters one item at a time and ask a child to place it in the box that shows the corresponding type of weather. Talk about why the various items are worn or used in each type of weather. After the sorting is finished, place the items in your dramatic-play area for youngsters to use independently.

hot   cold   rainy

Storytime

Reading Up a Storm

The forecast calls for good books galore at storytime! Add to your weather theme by donning sunglasses, a rain hat, or a pair of woolly mittens as you share some of these selections!

It's Raining, It's Pouring
By Kin Eagle

What Can You Do in the Rain?
What Can You Do in the Sun?
What Can You Do in the Snow?
All by Anna Grossnickle Hines

What's the Weather Today?
By Allan Fowler

Rain
By Robert Kalan

The Wind Blew
By Pat Hutchins

The Snowy Day
By Ezra Jack Keats

We like the sun. It's lots of fun!

We like the snow. It's cool, you know!

We like raindrops. We think they're tops!

Math Activity

Picture-Perfect Weather

Different people enjoy different types of weather. What kind of weather do *your* students like best? Find out when you create this display, which doubles as a weather-preference chart. Begin by dividing a bulletin board into three sections. Label each section with the weather icon and rhyme shown. Next, gather a pair of sunglasses, a pair of mittens and a scarf, and a child's umbrella. Ask one child at a time to tell you which of the three types of weather she likes best. Then take an instant photo of her dressed for that weather. After everyone has voted, post the photos in the appropriate sections of the bulletin board. Gather your little ones around to view the photos. As a class, count the number of children who prefer each type of weather. What's the favorite weather in your classroom?

Science Activity

Weather Wheels

Is the weather outside frightful or delightful? Your young weather watchers can make a daily report to their families with the help of these weather wheels. To prepare, duplicate page 119 to make a class supply. Have a child color the wedges on his copy as desired before cutting them out. Direct him to glue the four wedges to a white paper plate as shown. Then help him cut out the arrow and attach it to the center of the plate with a metal brad. Encourage little ones to take their weather wheels home and post them in a prominent place. Each day, a child can report on the weather he observes by pointing the arrow to the corresponding section on the wheel.

115

Weather Tunes

Start each day of your weather unit with a sing-along! These kid-friendly ditties cover the weather from sunny to stormy, and the motions and special effects will have your weather watchers wiggling and giggling!

Sunshine
(sung to the tune of "You Are My Sunshine")

Outside there's sunshine.   *Use arms to form circle sun overhead.*
There's lots of sunshine.   *Use arms to form circle sun overhead.*
And not a cloud in
The sky so blue!   *Shade eyes and look upward.*
So let's go outside!   *Point thumb toward door.*
Let's not stay inside!   *Shake index finger "no."*
I'll spend my sunny days with you!   *Point to self, then others.*

Pam Crane

Do You Love the Snow?
(sung to the tune of "Do Your Ears Hang Low?")

Do you love the snow?   *Put both hands over heart.*
You can play in it, you know!   *Point to others.*
You can make a big snowball   *Use both hands to form big circle.*
Or a snowman really tall!   *Indicate "tall" with one hand.*
You can travel on your skis,   *Pretend to grip ski poles and move hips.*
Make an angel if you please!   *Wave both arms as if making snow angel.*
Do you love the snow?   *Put both hands over heart.*

Lightning and Thunder

Give each child a flashlight and an aluminum pie pan to use for the sight and sound effects in this song. Dim your classroom lights to get the stormy mood just right!

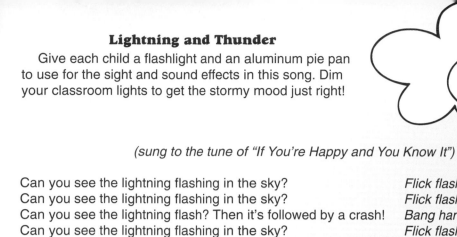

(sung to the tune of "If You're Happy and You Know It")

Can you see the lightning flashing in the sky?	*Flick flashlight on and off.*
Can you see the lightning flashing in the sky?	*Flick flashlight on and off.*
Can you see the lightning flash? Then it's followed by a crash!	*Bang hand against pie pan.*
Can you see the lightning flashing in the sky?	*Flick flashlight on and off.*

I Love Windy Weather
(sung to the tune of "I'm a Little Teapot")

I love windy weather!	*Put both hands over heart.*
See it blow.	*Shade eyes and look around.*
Watch the trees move to and fro.	*Put both arms up and sway body.*
Feel it on my face and in my hair.	*Touch hands to face, then hair.*
How I love that playful air!	*Put both hands over heart.*

117

Weather Art

Rain, clouds, snow, and sun—making all types of weather is really fun! And your youngsters can easily make this craft, which shows all four of these weather conditions. To begin, fold a sheet of white construction paper into four equal columns. Have each child follow the directions below to complete her project. When the paint and glue are dry, send these crafts home to prompt discussions about weather.

First column: Press on blue tempera paint fingerprints to make rain.

Second column: Color the space blue; then glue on bits of white paper doilies to make snow.

Third column: Sponge-paint a yellow circle sun in the center; then add rays with gold glitter glue.

Fourth column: Color the space gray; then glue on torn pieces of cotton balls for clouds.

Snack Activity

Sunny or Snowy Snacks

After crafting the project in "Weather Art," your little ones will enjoy visiting your snack table to create these edible weather pictures! Have each child choose to make either a sunny or a snowy snack. Then guide him through the preparations. Serve sunny snacks with cups of ice-cold lemonade. Serve snowy snacks with cups of warm milk. Yum!

Sunny Snack

graham cracker
blue-tinted frosting
vanilla wafer
yellow decorator icing

Frost the graham cracker with blue frosting to make the sky. Place the vanilla wafer in the center of the graham cracker. Squeeze icing from the tube to create rays for the cookie sun.

Snowy Snack

graham cracker
blue-tinted frosting
white sprinkles

Frost the graham cracker with blue frosting to make the sky. Add sprinkles all over the graham cracker to resemble snowflakes.

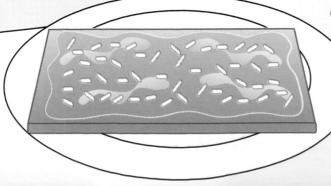

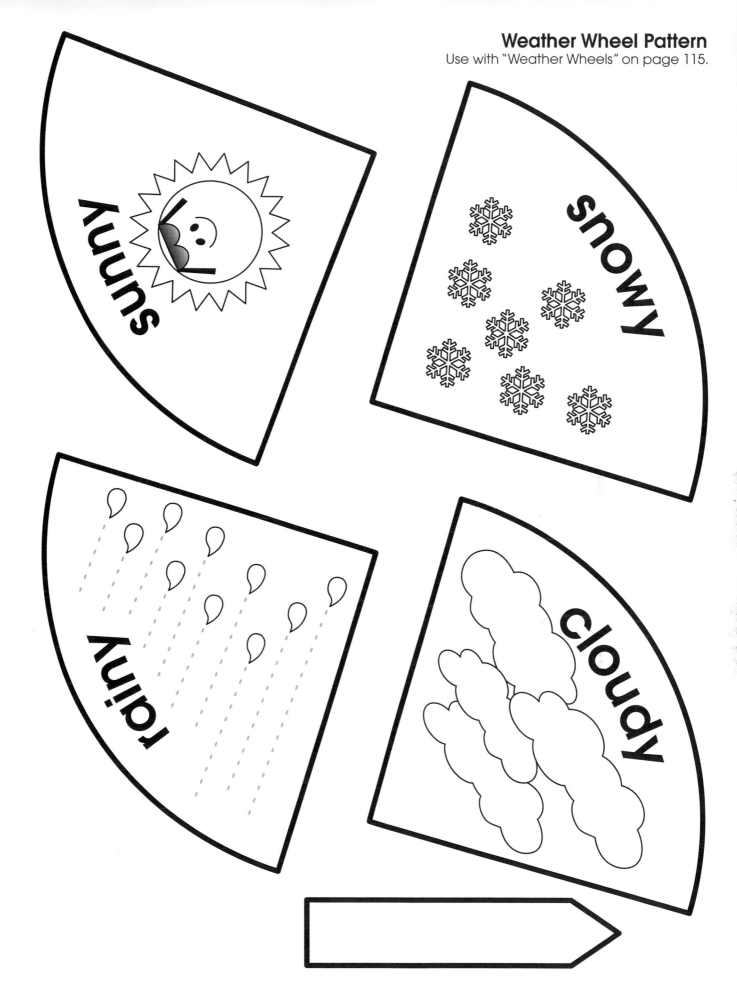

sunny

snowy

rainy

cloudy

'Twas the Night Before...

Christmas, Hanukkah, and Kwanzaa! With all the hustle and bustle, the holidays must be around the corner! So use the ideas on the following pages to introduce your little ones to a variety of seasonal symbols, treats, and traditions. Happy holidays!

ideas contributed by Lucia Kemp Henry and Suzanne Moore

...Christmas

Invite your youngsters to participate in these Christmas preparations and they're sure to learn a "ho, ho, ho" lot!

Craft

Oh, Christmas Tree!

The celebration of Christmas wouldn't be complete without a decorated tree. Use this craft idea and invite each child to create a miniature tree of her own. To make one, use pinking shears to cut out two four-inch-tall green tagboard tree shapes. Sandwich a craft stick by taping it to one shape and then gluing the other shape on top of it as shown. Invite a child to decorate the tagboard tree with holiday stickers, sticky dots, and glitter glue. When the glue is dry, help the child insert the craft stick into a Styrofoam ball half. Display your youngsters' trees on a table; then add cotton batting around the base of each tree to create a winter wonderland.

The Stockings Were Hung by the Chimney With Care

Hanging stockings is a sure sign that Christmas is fast approaching! With this idea, your youngsters will get into the spirit of the season while developing spatial-reasoning and fine-motor skills. Place three self-adhesive hooks on a wall in a center. Set three different-size stockings in the area along with toys in various sizes. Invite your little ones to discover which toys will fit into which stockings; then have them hang the stockings on the hooks. Encourage older students to hang the stockings in sequence from smallest to largest. It's beginning to look a lot like Christmas!

Center Idea

Cookies for Santa

One of the most important Christmas preparations is making sure a snack is available for jolly ol' St. Nick! Set up this center and have students prepare plates of craft-foam cookies for Santa. Place a large and a small paper plate at a center. Then cut out and decorate large and small craft-foam gingerbread cookies. Place the cookies in a container and set it at the center along with the plates. Invite each child to sort the cookies by size onto the appropriate plate. For added learning fun, set some crayons and paper near the center and encourage youngsters to write a note to Mr. Claus. Cookies and a note for Santa! No wonder he's so jolly!

Snack

Reindeer Toast

Santa's reindeer work hard on Christmas Eve. So invite each child to salute Rudolph and company by making a reindeer toast! To make one, toast a piece of bread; then spread peanut butter over it. Use a plastic knife to cut the bread and arrange the pieces as shown. Then add two raisin eyes, a maraschino cherry half nose, and pretzel stick antlers. With this snack idea, you're likely to hear little ones saying, "Excuse me, I'd like to make a toast…."

121

...Hanukkah

Your youngsters will be all aglow as they participate in these Hanukkah-themed activities.

Group Activity

Hanukkah Is Here!

To prepare for this circle-time activity, follow the directions in "Lovely Lights" (below) to create a class menorah. Assemble the menorah without the paper flames; then display it in your circle-time area. To begin the activity, place a paper flame in the *shammash* and sing the song shown. Then provide a child with a paper flame and direct him to place it in the first candle. At the end of the day, remove the flames from the candles. Repeat the activity the following day, adding one more flame and singing the song accordingly. Continue the activity each day until all eight candles are lit. On certain days, light more than one candle for those days when students will not be in school.

*The **shammash** is the tallest candle on the menorah and is used to light the other candles.*

(sung to the tune of "For He's a Jolly Good Fellow")

It's time to light the candles.
It's time to light the candles.
It's time to light the candles,
For Hannukah is here!

For Hannukah is here!
For Hannukah is here!
It's time to light the candles,
For Hannukah is here!

Let's light [one] pretty candle(s).
Let's light [one] pretty candle(s).
Let's light [one] pretty candle(s),
For this special time of year!

Center Idea

Lovely Lights

One cup, one candle, one flame. Reinforce one-to-one correspondence with this center idea, which has youngsters assembling a pretend menorah. To prepare, use the pattern on page 126 to make nine construction paper flames. Paint eight toilet paper tubes blue. To make the shammash, cut a paper towel tube in half and paint one of the halves blue. When the paint is dry, place each tube inside a nine-ounce paper cup wrapped in foil. To make a menorah, line up the cups as shown with the shammash in the middle. Invite students to light the menorah by placing one flame inside each tube. For older students, separate the cups, candles, and flames. Then direct them to assemble the menorah by placing a tube in each cup and a flame in each tube.

Love Those Latkes!

Potato latkes are a traditional Hanukkah treat. Try this simplified recipe and give your youngsters a taste of Jewish tradition.

Easy Latkes
(makes 10 pancakes)

Ingredients:

2 c. packed frozen shredded hash browns
3 eggs, beaten
1 tbsp. flour
1 tbsp. plain bread crumbs
1 tsp. salt
½ c. oil

Spread the hash browns on a clean cutting board to thaw. Pat the thawed hash browns dry with a paper towel. Mix the hash browns, eggs, flour, bread crumbs, and salt in a bowl. In a large skillet over medium heat, heat the oil until hot. Drop tablespoons of the mixture into the oil; then gently press them with a spatula to make ¼-inch-thick pancakes. Brown the pancakes on one side; then flip them over and brown the other side. Drain the pancakes on paper towels. If desired, serve with applesauce or sour cream.

On the Hunt for Hanukkah Gifts

Eight days of Hanukkah means eight small gifts for little ones! Stir up a little excitement at your sensory table by filling it with foam packing pieces and then hiding eight small gift wrapped boxes in the table. Invite your youngsters to search for the boxes and then sort them by size, wrapping paper, or bows. Or program each box with a different number from 1 to 8 and have students place the boxes in numerical order. There are a whole lot of learning opportunities wrapped up in this center!

Gelt Guessing

Gelt, the Yiddish word for money, also refers to chocolate coins that many children receive during Hanukkah. This estimation activity has students preparing pretend sacks of gelt for the giving! In advance, make several yellow copies of the gelt patterns on page 126. Laminate the patterns. Cut them out and then place a self-adhesive magnetic strip on the back of each one. Next, photocopy the sack patterns on page 127. Cut out the sacks and then tape them onto a magnetic board or a cookie sheet. Place the coins around the sacks; then display the board in your circle-time area. To begin the activity, invite students to guess how many coins will fit onto the smallest sack. Place the coins on the sack and then count them with your youngsters. Continue in this manner with the medium-size sack and the large sack. After completing the activity, open up a real sack of Hanukkah gelt and treat each child to a tasty gold foil–wrapped chocolate coin. Happy Hanukkah!

···Kwanzaa

This colorful collection of Kwanzaa ideas is just right for a preschool celebration!

Group Activity

The Colors of Kwanzaa

Use this group activity to help youngsters become familiar with the traditional colors of Kwanzaa—red, black, and green. To begin, teach youngsters the song below. Then provide each child with a red, black, or green streamer. After naming a Kwanzaa color, have students with that color streamer sing the song and wave their streamers in the air. Continue the activity until all the colors of Kwanzaa have been named.

(sung to the tune of "Jingle Bells")

Colors bold, colors bright
Shine this time of year!
The color [black] is all around,
For Kwanzaa time is here!

Repeat, replacing the underlined word in turn with *red* and *green*.

Display

Umoja Means "Unity"

One of the principles of Kwanzaa is *umoja* (oo-MOH-jah), or unity. Invite little hands to unite and create a class Kwanzaa flag. To prepare, place shallow pans of black, green, and red paint on a newspaper-covered table. Have each child make several handprints in each color on a large sheet of bulletin board paper as shown. When the paint is dry, display the completed flag in your classroom as a festive reminder of umoja.

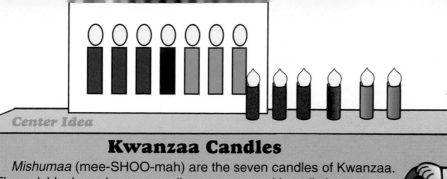

Kwanzaa Candles

Mishumaa (mee-SHOO-mah) are the seven candles of Kwanzaa. The red, black, and green candles are arranged in a distinct pattern on the *kinara,* the Kwanzaa candleholder. Set up this center to help your youngsters become familiar with the mishumaa and also to reinforce visual-discrimination and color-matching skills. In advance, collect seven toilet paper tubes. Paint three tubes red, three tubes green, and one tube black. When the paint is dry, tape a construction paper flame to the inside of each painted tube so that it resembles a candle. Display a color picture of a kinara at the center; then set the candles near the picture. Invite each child to use the picture to guide him as he places the Kwanzaa candles in the proper pattern.

Cooking

Sesame Sweets

Benne cakes are a popular Kwanzaa treat with a special ingredient for good luck—sesame seeds! If you have a parent who enjoys baking, enlist his help in making these tasty treats for your students to sample.

Benne Cakes
(makes approximately 24 cakes)

Ingredients:

nonstick cooking spray
1 c. brown sugar
¼ c. softened butter
1 beaten egg
½ tsp. vanilla

1 tsp. lemon juice
½ c. flour
½ tsp. baking powder
¼ tsp. salt
¾ c. sesame seeds

Preheat the oven to 325°. Lightly oil the cookie sheet. Mix brown sugar and butter until creamy. Stir in the egg, vanilla, and lemon juice. Then mix in the remaining ingredients. Drop the batter by rounded teaspoons about two inches apart on a cookie sheet. Bake for about 15 minutes or until the edges are browned.

Craft

In Kwanzaa tradition, ears of corn are symbolic of children; one ear represents one child.

A Gift of Corn

Kwanzaa gifts, called *zawadi,* are often handmade. Invite each child to create a crafty ear of corn to give to a special someone. To make one, press orange and brown paint fingerprints onto a 4" x 1½" yellow craft-foam corn shape. Next, glue a few small crepe paper pieces to the end of a jumbo craft stick. Then use craft glue to attach the stick to the back of the corn so the crepe paper resembles the husk. Place a self-adhesive magnetic strip on the stick and the gift is complete!

Flame Pattern
Use with "Hanukkah Is Here!" and "Lovely Lights" on page 122.

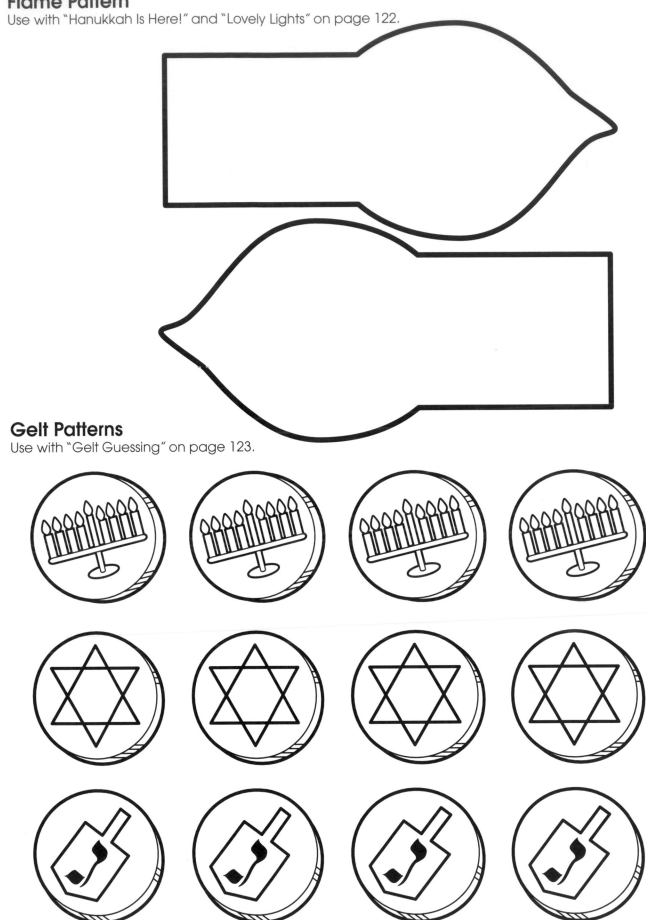

Gelt Patterns
Use with "Gelt Guessing" on page 123.

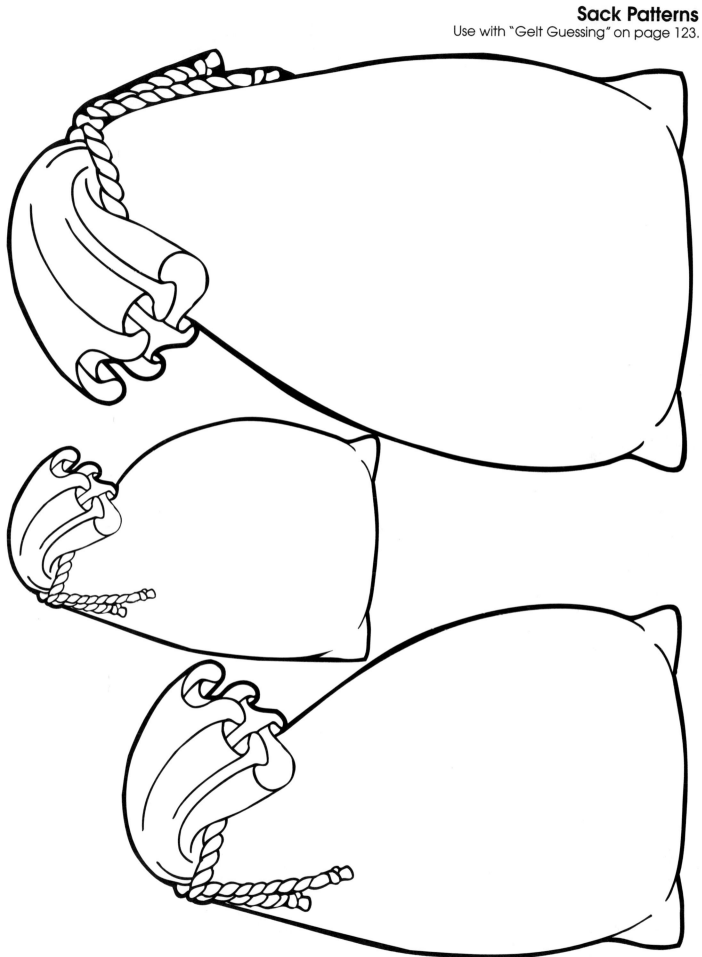

To Market, to Market

Shopping for new center ideas? Stock your learning centers with grocery-related activities that feed the need for preschool learning fun!

by Angie Kutzer

Attention, All Shoppers!

Enlist co-workers, relatives, friends, and students' parents to collect enough materials for the ideas in this unit. Make sure to request that the food containers be emptied and cleaned before being sent in.

— food boxes, bags, and cans
— milk or juice cartons (a supply that is the same size, quart or larger)
— paper grocery bags
— boxes of cereal rings (such as Cheerios, Froot Loops, or Apple Jacks cereal pieces) to fill your sensory table and for snacking
— grocery store ads
— coupon sections from newspapers
— discarded food and household magazines (such as *Cooking Light, Good Housekeeping,* and *Woman's Day*)
— novelty toys to use as prizes (optional)

food boxes
bags
cans
milk cartons
juice cartons

TACO CHIPS

COLORFUL WAFERS

CHOCO Pudding

Literacy Center
Shopping Lists

With a little preparation, you can help your students load up on literacy skills. In advance, cut off the front panels of several food packages and put them in a pile. Make shopping lists by cutting out the brand names from the leftover packaging and gluing groups of them onto different sheets of paper as shown. Staple each list onto a paper grocery bag. To complete the activity, instruct a child to read a list and fill the bag with the correct items. If desired, have a partner check the child's work by unloading the bag. Now the center is ready for the next shoppers.

Pam Crane

Bag It!

Math is in the bag with this nonstandard-measurement activity. Stock the math center with a supply of milk or juice cartons that are the same size (quart or larger). You'll also need to include a paper grocery bag and a canvas grocery bag. Have each shopper who visits the center estimate how many cartons the paper bag will hold. Then instruct her to count as she fills the paper bag. Now encourage the child to predict which bag will hold more: the paper or the canvas. Direct her to fill the canvas bag and compare the results. What a bagful of learning!

Taste Tests

Conduct a few taste tests during your grocery store unit to give your little consumers practice with graphing. Make a simple two-column graph and laminate it. Use a washable marker to program the graph as shown. Provide taste samples for each student and then have him record his preference on the graph. Discuss the results during a later group time. Try a new test each day!

Possible taste tests:
Coke soda vs. Pepsi soda
name brand vs. generic brand
chocolate chip cookie vs.
    sugar cookie
fresh fruit vs. dehydrated fruit
tomato soup vs. chicken noodle soup

Which do you prefer?	
chocolate chip	sugar
Hunter	Evan
Torie	Jill
Cassidy	
Ross	

Water Table
Catch of the Day

Ask a child what he likes to see at the grocery store, and the lobster tank is sure to be on his list. Use a copy of the lobster patterns on page 132 to make a supply of craft foam cutouts. Use different colors of foam or use a permanent marker to program pairs of lobsters with matching letters, shapes, or numbers. Put the lobsters in your water table along with several pairs of tongs. Invite youngsters to use the tongs to catch all the lobsters and then find matching pairs or sort them. Get your fresh seafood right here!

Blocks Center
Dazzling Displays

Your youngsters will exercise their problem-solving skills as they pretend to be store stockers in this building activity. Put a large supply of cans, plastic bottles, and boxes in your blocks center. Each day, give the students in the center a cardboard base that's different in shape or size. Encourage the stockers to work together to create a product display that uses as many of the empty food packages as possible. "Tower-ific!"

Fine-Motor Center
Snip, Snip, Snip!

Scissor skills get checked out at this fun center. Have youngsters look through a variety of grocery advertisements, coupon sections of newspapers, and magazines that contain grocery coupons. As each child finds products that her family uses, encourage her to cut out the correlating coupons and take them home. Or have students cut out all the coupons they find and then set them out for parents to pick from. Preschoolers get cutting practice and parents get to save money. Now *that's* a bargain!

Art Center

That's My Name

Take advantage of all the environmental print coming into your room to reinforce letter and name recognition. To prepare, cut apart paper grocery bags so that each child can have the front or back panel of one. Direct the child to look at a supply of food packages (and the leftover ads from "Snip, Snip, Snip!" on page 130) to find the letters in her name. Have her cut out the letters, arrange them to spell her name, and glue them onto her paper. Then encourage her to add pictures of foods she likes to eat to make a collage. Display the finished projects on a board titled "We Are What We Eat!" Yummy!

Sensory Table

Cereal Surprises

Turn your sensory table into one big cereal bowl to provide your youngsters with an opportunity to explore. Fill the table with several boxes of cereal rings, such as Froot Loops, Cheerios, or Apple Jacks cereal pieces. Provide scoops, large spoons, measuring cups, and yarn lengths for youngsters to use to work on measurement and patterning concepts. For added fun, hide novelty toys in the cereal for students to find. Be sure to have some "untouched" cereal nearby for kids who want to crunch and munch!

Lobster Pattern
Use with "Catch of the Day" on page 130.

GET HEART HAPPY!

Hearts are everywhere at this time of year, so go ahead—bring them into your classroom, too! Heart shapes will be a "love-ly" way for your preschoolers to learn about math, science, music, and more!

by Ada Goren

CRAFT DISPLAY

A "HEART-Y" WELCOME

Let everyone know about the heart hoopla in your class with this door decoration idea! Mount the title shown on or near your classroom door. Then encourage your preschoolers to create hearts at your art center to add to the display. Set out precut construction paper hearts, heart-shaped paper doilies, heart stickers, craft foam hearts, and a variety of papers, markers, glue, crayons, and other craft materials. Invite youngsters to freely design hearts each day during your center time; then display their original creations around your door. Keep the heart art going throughout your unit, and keep adding students' creations to the door display. Little ones will be so proud!

We Welcome You With All Our Hearts!

SONG

LITTLE RED HEARTS

Teach youngsters this simple song and invite them to play along with the help of their ten fingers! Before singing, affix a red heart sticker to each of a child's ten fingertips. Or use a washable marker to draw a red heart on each one. Then have each student hold up one finger at a time as the song progresses. At the end, have children wiggle those little red hearts!

(sung to the tune of "Ten Little Indians")

One little, two little, three little red hearts,
Four little, five little, six little red hearts,
Seven little, eight little, nine little red hearts,
Ten little wiggling red hearts!

SORTING

THIS IS SORT OF FUN

Big or little, red or pink, lacy or ruffled—hearts can be just about any size, color, or design! Use the heart patterns on page 138 to sharpen your preschoolers' sorting skills. Duplicate the patterns on three different colors of paper. Then cut out all the hearts and laminate them for durability. Store the hearts in a zippered plastic bag (or a heart-shaped candy box) and put it at your math center. Have a child at this center take the hearts out of the bag and sort them as she wishes—by color, by size, or by design.

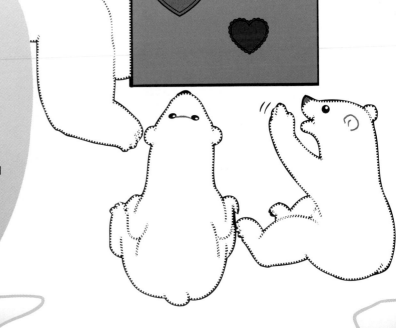

VISUAL MEMORY

MISSING!

Use the same reproducible hearts created for "This Is Sort of Fun" at your flannelboard to improve little ones' visual memory. Use masking tape to place three to five of the heart cutouts on your flannelboard. Ask youngsters to look at them for about 30 seconds. Then have students close their eyes as you remove one of the hearts and put it out of sight. Have youngsters open their eyes and try to determine which heart is missing from the flannelboard. Invite the student who correctly identifies the missing heart to remove another heart from the board in the next round.

GET THOSE HEARTS PUMPING!

Get your preschoolers' real hearts pumping with the help of a heart shape outlined on your classroom floor. Use masking tape to outline a large heart shape on the floor. (Make it large enough for your whole group to stand inside it.) Then teach little ones the song shown and have them move as you direct in the second line of each verse. Substitute various gross-motor movements—such as *walk, sidestep, hop,* or *twist*—for the underlined action words.

(sung to the tune of "The Farmer in the Dell")

Inside the heart, inside the heart,
[Tiptoe, tiptoe],
Inside the heart!

Outside the heart, outside the heart,
[Jump, jump, jump, jump],
Outside the heart!

HEALTH/NUTRITION

HEALTHY HEARTS

Explain to your students that moving and exercising (as they did in "Get Those Hearts Pumping!") is very good for their real hearts. Duplicate the chart on page 139 and post it in your classroom. Each day for a week, lead your students in an exercise routine that'll get their little hearts working! When the session is complete, stick a heart-shaped sticker in the box for that day. When the week is over and all the boxes are filled with heart stickers, reward each child with a badge duplicated from page 139. Then invite the whole class to enjoy a heart-healthy snack, such as graham crackers or air-popped popcorn!

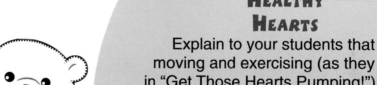

HIDDEN HEARTS

"I found one!" That's what you'll hear as youngsters discover the craft foam heart shapes hidden in your sensory table. Simply cut a supply of heart shapes from various colors of craft foam. Scatter them in your sensory table; then cover them with red and pink crinkled gift wrap stuffing or pink and purple Easter grass. Invite children at this center to uncover the hidden hearts. For an added challenge, create a stack of number cards to keep near your sensory table. Have a child draw a card and then try to find a corresponding number of hearts.

CENTER IDEAS

CANDY BOX CHAOS

Collect heart-shaped candy boxes to add a "heart-y" touch to your classroom centers!

Manipulatives Area: Provide the tops and bottoms of candy boxes in various sizes and designs. Have youngsters match the tops to the bottoms.

Blocks Center: Encourage youngsters to add heart-shaped boxes to their building fun!

Play Dough Center: Have youngsters create play dough confections to fill a box. Or use smaller boxes as cutters for creating heart-shaped cookies and cakes.

Literacy Area: Gather a collection of objects or pictures, some that begin with the letter *H* and some that do not. Put a heart-shaped box in the center and ask youngsters to fill it with items that begin with *H*, like *heart*.

Painting Easel: Use the top and bottom of a large heart-shaped box as printers to make both heart outlines and solid hearts.

CRAFT

LOVELY LOCKETS

Craft these construction paper lockets for youngsters to give as Valentine's Day gifts! For each child, fold a 3" x 6" piece of red construction paper into a 3" x 3" square. Cut a heart shape on the fold. In advance, have students bring in small pictures of loved ones, or gather a small picture of each child.

To make a locket, tie the ends of a 24-inch length of red yarn to make a necklace. Tape the center of the necklace to the back of the heart cutout. Next, have a child glue her photo inside the locket. When the glue is dry, invite her to use glitter glue to decorate the front of her locket; then allow the glitter glue to dry thoroughly. Finally, to keep the locket closed, put a tiny bit of Sticky-Tac adhesive inside the locket. The locket will stay closed when being worn and can be easily pulled open to reveal the photo inside.

SNACK

A SHAPELY SNACK

Think pink to prepare this heart-shaped snack little ones will love! For each child, toast a slice of bread. Have the child use a large heart-shaped cookie cutter to cut a heart shape from the toast. Then have him spread strawberry cream cheese over the toast before sprinkling on some heart-shaped sprinkles! And what better to accompany this toasty heart snack than a pink drink? Prepare a cup of milk mixed with strawberry Nesquik drink mix for each snacker. Make the sipping special by attaching a craft foam heart shape to each child's drinking straw (as shown). Mmm… these hearts are sure to make 'em happy!

Heart Patterns

Use with "This Is Sort of Fun" and "Missing!" on page 134.

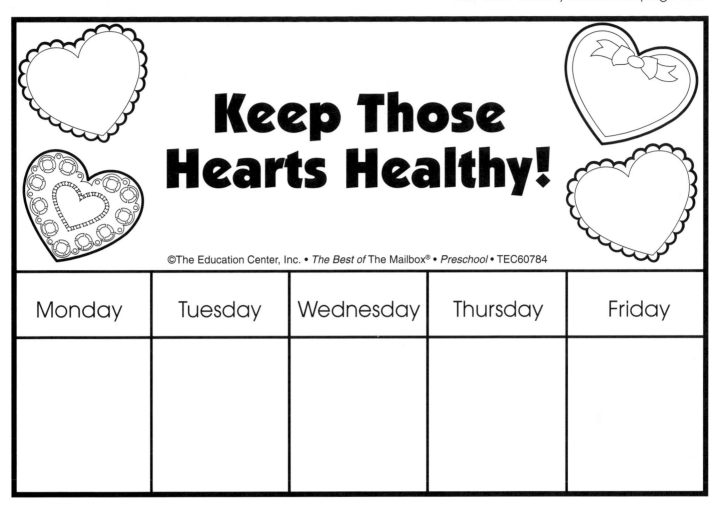

Keep Those Hearts Healthy!

Monday	Tuesday	Wednesday	Thursday	Friday

I Keep My Heart Healthy!

Ask Me How!

Every Chick Counts

Need some math ideas that you can count on? Use this collection of chick-themed activities and teaching math skills will be as easy as 1, 2, 3!

ideas by Sue Fleischmann—Preschool, Holy Cross School, Menomonee Falls, WI

Here a Chick, There a Chick

Going on a chick hunt is a great way to motivate youngsters and get them counting! In advance, use the pattern on page 143 to make a supply of chick cutouts. Be sure to make enough chicks for each child to have at least one. Then hide the chicks throughout your classroom. For added fun, scatter a few yellow craft feathers around the room. To begin the activity, show students a paper chick and explain that several more chicks are hiding in the classroom. Play some lively music and invite your youngsters to search for the remaining chicks. When the music stops, bring your group together to count each child's chicks. If desired, make a graph similar to the one shown. Have each child place his chicks on the graph. Then use terms such as *more, less,* and *equal* to discuss what the graph reveals. ***counting, comparing numbers of objects, vocabulary***

Counting Chicks

Kate	Tara	Nick	Teddy	Christy

Bouncing Baby Chicks

A few old tennis balls and a parachute are all you need to put some bounce into a counting lesson. In advance, use paint pens to draw eyes, wings, and a beak on each ball. When the paint is dry, have each child hold the edge of a parachute. Place the tennis ball chicks in the middle of the parachute. Sing the song shown and have youngsters shake the parachute to make the chicks "hop." After singing the last line, invite a child to say a number. Have the class count out loud as they shake the parachute and make the chicks "hop" that many times. Continue the activity until each child has had a chance to say a number.
meaningful counting, gross-motor skills

(sung to the tune of "The Wheels on the Bus")

Little baby chicks hop up and down,
Up and down,
Up and down.
Little baby chicks hop up and down.
How many times?

Little Chick, Little Chick

There's nothing like an entertaining action poem to get your little chicks cheeping! To prepare for this activity, use the pattern on page 143 to make five chick necklaces, each labeled with a different number from 1 to 5. During your group time, invite five children to stand in front of the class. Provide each child with a chick necklace and identify its number. As you recite the poem below, have each little chick perform an action as directed in the poem. *number recognition, listening, gross-motor skills*

Little chick, little chick, number one,
Flap your wings and have some fun.
Little chick, little chick, number two,
Reach way down and touch your shoe.
Little chick, little chick, number three,
Nod your head for us to see.
Little chick, little chick, number four,
Jump up high, right off the floor.
Little chick, little chick number five,
Dance around and do the jive.

Chicks Ahoy!

Keep math skills afloat with this water table idea. To prepare, use permanent markers to draw beaks, eyes, and wings on each of 15 Ping-Pong balls. Place the Ping-Pong ball chicks in a container and then set it near your water table. Next, label the sides of five small plastic margarine tubs, each with a different number from 1 to 5. If desired, also program the inside of each tub with a corresponding set of dots. Float the tubs in the water table. To use the center, a child reads the numeral on each tub and then places the correct number of chicks in it. Rub-a-dub-dub! The chicks are in the tub! *number recognition, creating sets to match numbers*

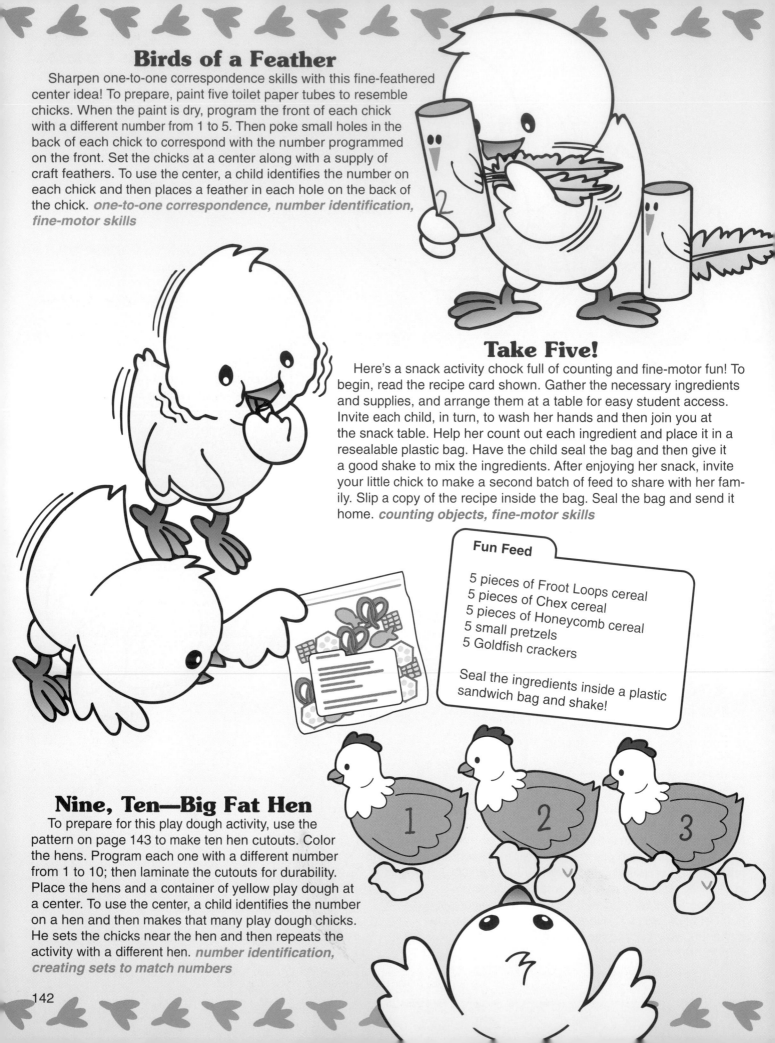

Birds of a Feather

Sharpen one-to-one correspondence skills with this fine-feathered center idea! To prepare, paint five toilet paper tubes to resemble chicks. When the paint is dry, program the front of each chick with a different number from 1 to 5. Then poke small holes in the back of each chick to correspond with the number programmed on the front. Set the chicks at a center along with a supply of craft feathers. To use the center, a child identifies the number on each chick and then places a feather in each hole on the back of the chick. *one-to-one correspondence, number identification, fine-motor skills*

Take Five!

Here's a snack activity chock full of counting and fine-motor fun! To begin, read the recipe card shown. Gather the necessary ingredients and supplies, and arrange them at a table for easy student access. Invite each child, in turn, to wash her hands and then join you at the snack table. Help her count out each ingredient and place it in a resealable plastic bag. Have the child seal the bag and then give it a good shake to mix the ingredients. After enjoying her snack, invite your little chick to make a second batch of feed to share with her family. Slip a copy of the recipe inside the bag. Seal the bag and send it home. *counting objects, fine-motor skills*

Fun Feed

5 pieces of Froot Loops cereal
5 pieces of Chex cereal
5 pieces of Honeycomb cereal
5 small pretzels
5 Goldfish crackers

Seal the ingredients inside a plastic sandwich bag and shake!

Nine, Ten—Big Fat Hen

To prepare for this play dough activity, use the pattern on page 143 to make ten hen cutouts. Color the hens. Program each one with a different number from 1 to 10; then laminate the cutouts for durability. Place the hens and a container of yellow play dough at a center. To use the center, a child identifies the number on a hen and then makes that many play dough chicks. He sets the chicks near the hen and then repeats the activity with a different hen. *number identification, creating sets to match numbers*

Chick

Use with "Here a Chi[ck], Chick" on page 140 [and...] Chick, Little Chick" on [...]

Hen Pattern

Use with "Nine, Ten—Big Fat Hen" on page 142.

Counting Award

Cheep! Cheep! Hooray!

I practiced counting today!

Let me count to _____ for you.

©The Education Center, Inc. • *The Best of* The Mailbox® • *Preschool* • TEC60784

Note to the teacher: Make a class supply to express counting kudos.

Beautiful Butterflies

You're sure to be all aflutter over these butterfly ideas that glided in from our subscribers!

ideas contributed by preschool teachers from across the country

One Day a Caterpillar, the Next Day a Butterfly!

If you're looking for an easy and age-appropriate way to teach your children about the life cycle of a butterfly, just follow these steps. Invite each child to make a caterpillar by gluing several green pom-poms to a spring-type clothespin. Then have him dot eyes onto one of the pom-poms with a black marker. The second day, have each child put his caterpillar in a cardboard tube. Direct each child to wrap his tube in yarn to create a cocoon. The third day, have each child take his caterpillar out of its cocoon. Then have him tint a coffee filter with food coloring. When the filter is dry, clip it into the clothespin to create a butterfly. Now that the transformations have been made, sing the song at the right to reinforce the lesson on metamorphosis.

Beth Howell—Three-Year-Olds
Grace Lutheran, Key West, FL

Music to Change By

No child will turn down his chance to dramatize the change a caterpillar makes into a butterfly.
(sung to the tune of "Three Blind Mice")

[Three] caterpillars, [three] caterpillars,
See how they crawl? See how they crawl?
They roll up in a chrysalis,
And wait for metamorphosis,
A sight you wouldn't want to miss!
[Three] butterflies, [three] butterflies.

Debby Moon—Two- to Five-Year-Olds
School for Little People
Wichita Falls, TX

Mega Metamorphosis

Here's a flamboyant flutterer that will make your point about metamorphosis in a *big* way! To make a giant caterpillar, have each child paint one or more paper plates green. Paint an extra plate; then, when the paint is dry, add paper features to it to make a face. Staple the plates together in a row; then use yarn to hang the caterpillar from the ceiling. One day while your class is out of the room, attach lengths of cellophane wrap to both sides of the caterpillar and to the ceiling as shown to create a giant butterfly with colorful wings!

Joan Anthou, Just About Kids, McMurray, PA

B Is for Butterfly

Give me a *B!* What have ya got? A butterfly! Say it again. A butterfly. Yeah! Make a class supply of the pattern on page 149 on construction paper. Have each child cut out one letter and then decorate it using craft supplies, such as crayons, markers, tissue paper, watercolor paints, confetti, and more. Next, have each child use markers to draw facial features on one end of a large craft stick and write her name on the center of the stick. Finally, have each child glue her letter *B* onto her stick. B-b-b-beautiful!

Kate Buschur—Preschool, Village Childcare
Kettering, OH

"Confetti-fly"

These butterflies look stunning when they glide over to a sunny window and rest awhile there on display. But for added fun, have some of them flit over to the discovery center where youngsters can use magnifying glasses to study their wings. To make one butterfly, fold a piece of black construction paper in half lengthwise. Using white crayon or chalk, trace the butterfly pattern on page 148 onto the paper as indicated. Cut out the butterfly shape and the centers of its wings. Put the unfolded shape on a piece of clear Con-Tact paper. Sprinkle bug-themed or other shaped confetti onto the wings before pressing a second piece of Con-Tact paper onto the butterfly. Trim around the shape. To complete the project, punch a hole at the tip of the butterfly's body and twist on a black pipe cleaner for antennae.

Sally Hanvelt—Preschool
First Friends Child Care Center, Eau Claire, WI

Butterfly Plant Marker

Dress up potted plants with these butterfly markers. To make one, trace the butterfly pattern (page 149) onto a piece of craft foam once; then flip the pattern over and trace it again to complete the butterfly outline. Cut out the shape. Punch a hole in the top of the butterfly; then twist on a pipe cleaner for antennae. Embellish the butterfly by gluing on Wonderfoam Shapes. (These precut colorful shapes of craft foam are available from school supplies catalogs or at craft stores.) Finally, glue a craft stick to the bottom back of the butterfly. Insert the stick into a pot to decorate a plant.

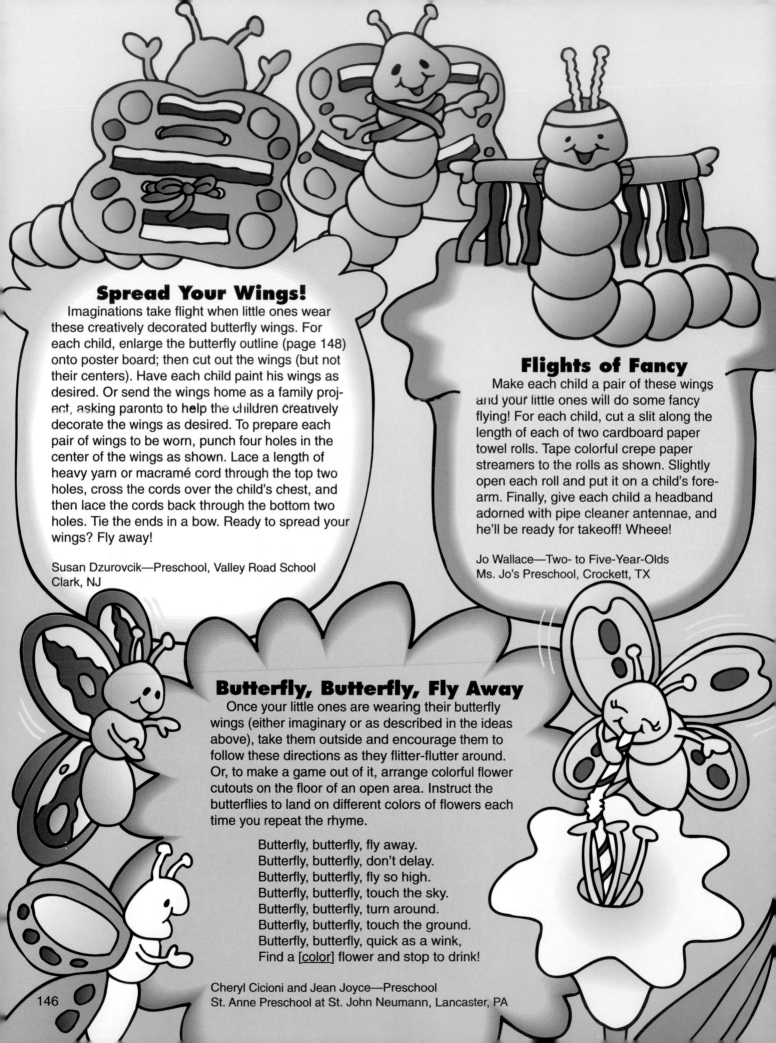

Spread Your Wings!

Imaginations take flight when little ones wear these creatively decorated butterfly wings. For each child, enlarge the butterfly outline (page 148) onto poster board; then cut out the wings (but not their centers). Have each child paint his wings as desired. Or send the wings home as a family project, asking parents to help the children creatively decorate the wings as desired. To prepare each pair of wings to be worn, punch four holes in the center of the wings as shown. Lace a length of heavy yarn or macramé cord through the top two holes, cross the cords over the child's chest, and then lace the cords back through the bottom two holes. Tie the ends in a bow. Ready to spread your wings? Fly away!

Susan Dzurovcik—Preschool, Valley Road School
Clark, NJ

Flights of Fancy

Make each child a pair of these wings and your little ones will do some fancy flying! For each child, cut a slit along the length of each of two cardboard paper towel rolls. Tape colorful crepe paper streamers to the rolls as shown. Slightly open each roll and put it on a child's forearm. Finally, give each child a headband adorned with pipe cleaner antennae, and he'll be ready for takeoff! Wheee!

Jo Wallace—Two- to Five-Year-Olds
Ms. Jo's Preschool, Crockett, TX

Butterfly, Butterfly, Fly Away

Once your little ones are wearing their butterfly wings (either imaginary or as described in the ideas above), take them outside and encourage them to follow these directions as they flitter-flutter around. Or, to make a game out of it, arrange colorful flower cutouts on the floor of an open area. Instruct the butterflies to land on different colors of flowers each time you repeat the rhyme.

Butterfly, butterfly, fly away.
Butterfly, butterfly, don't delay.
Butterfly, butterfly, fly so high.
Butterfly, butterfly, touch the sky.
Butterfly, butterfly, turn around.
Butterfly, butterfly, touch the ground.
Butterfly, butterfly, quick as a wink,
Find a [color] flower and stop to drink!

Cheryl Cicioni and Jean Joyce—Preschool
St. Anne Preschool at St. John Neumann, Lancaster, PA

Bit o' Butterfly

No butterfly study is complete without a butterfly-themed snack. To make one of these treats, slice a piece of toast in half diagonally. Spread jelly on both pieces of toast; then arrange colored sprinkles on top. Or spread flavored cream cheese on the toast; then top it with colorful round cereal pieces. Arrange the toast pieces and an oval-shaped cookie on a plate as shown. Finish the treat by adding licorice antennae and two cereal pieces (for eyes) to the cookie.

Loryl Fisher—Preschool
Happy Hands Methodist Preschool
Lemont, IL

Flutter By

To make one of these fantastic finger puppets, fold a 4" x 6" piece of card stock in half. Draw a butterfly wing on the fold; then cut it out, making sure to cut through both layers of paper but not through the fold. Cut two slits, about ¾" apart, perpendicular to the fold. Unfold the wings and then invite a child to decorate them with various craft supplies. When the butterfly is decorated, invite the child to slip one or two fingers through the slits. Use a marker to add a smiley face to the child's finger. Watch that butterfly fly away!

Molly Nagel
Cheshire, CT

Take a Dip, Take a Sip

What do butterflies do when they get thirsty? They sip nectar through their long, tube-shaped tongues! In this activity, your little ones can pretend to be butterflies as they dip straws into "nectar-filled flowers" and sip away. To make a class supply, duplicate the flower pattern (page 149) onto colorful construction paper; then cut out the flowers and their centers. Have each child use crayons to decorate his flower; then tape the underside of the flower onto the sides of a five-ounce cup as shown. Carefully fill the cup with fruit punch. Invite each child to pretend to be a butterfly as he uses his tongue (straw) to take a sip.

Debra Holbrook—Four-Year-Olds, SBEC, Olive Branch, MS

147

Pattern

Use with "'Confetti-fly'" on page 145 and "Spread Your Wings!" on page 146.

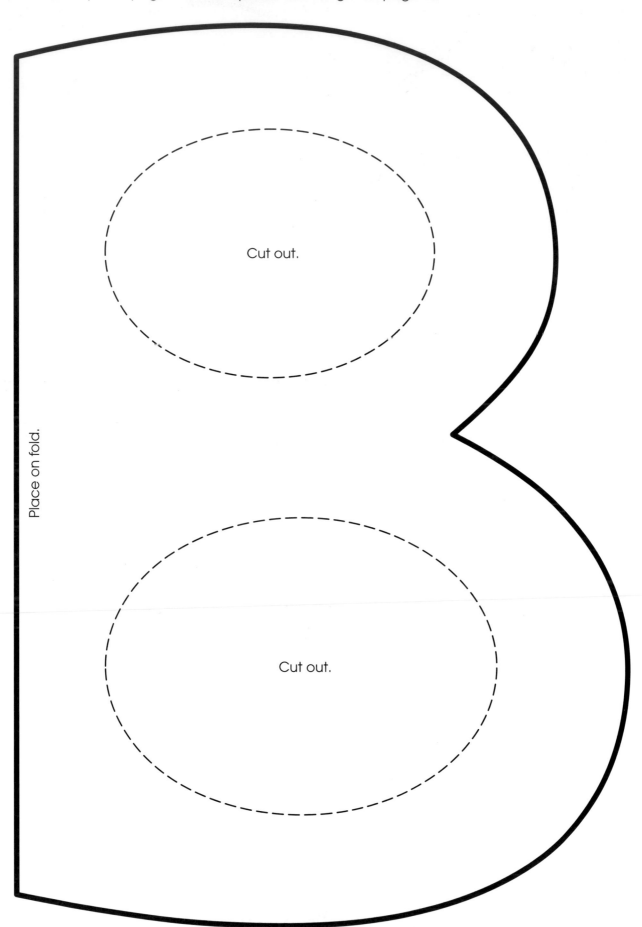

Cut out.

Place on fold.

Cut out.

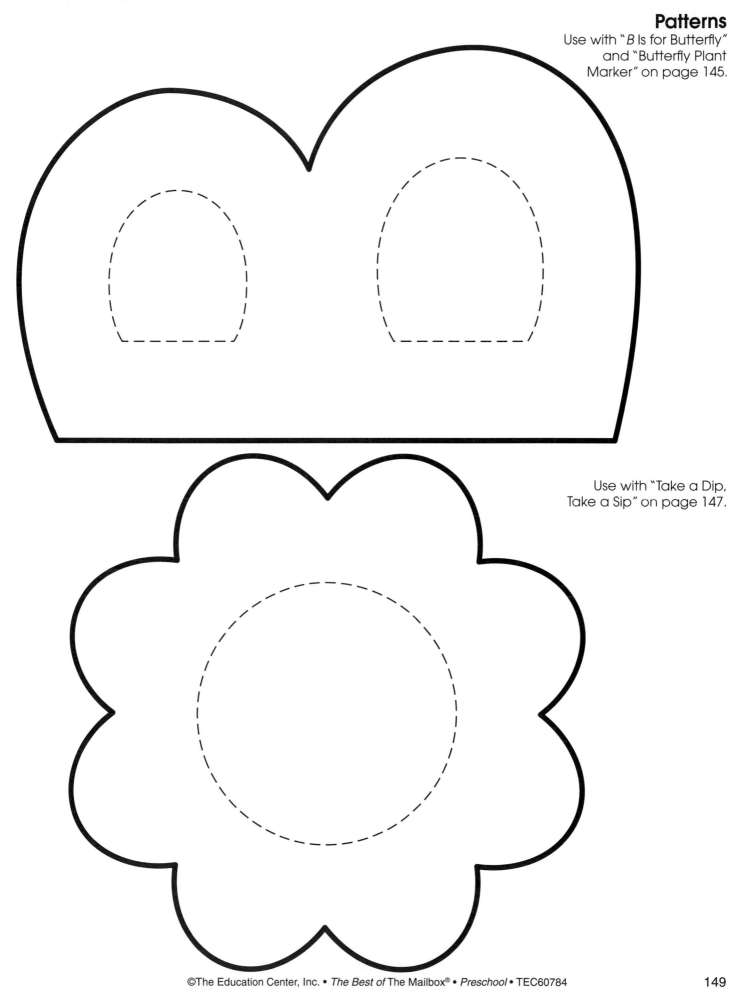

Patterns
Use with "*B* Is for Butterfly"
and "Butterfly Plant
Marker" on page 145.

Use with "Take a Dip,
Take a Sip" on page 147.

A "14-Carrot" Collection

What better way to celebrate the spring season than with a focus on the Easter Bunny's favorite food? Try these cute carrot ideas to put some crunch into your curriculum!

by Ada Goren

A Classic Carrot Story

Begin your concentration on carrots by sharing *The Carrot Seed* by Ruth Krauss. Afterward, provide a few props and guide your youngsters to act out this simple tale. Prepare by purchasing a packet of carrot seeds. Empty the packet; then laminate it for durability. Gather a plastic shovel, a watering can, and a child's wheelbarrow (or wagon). Check your local discount or party store to find a large inflatable carrot during the Easter season. Or make your own giant carrot! Simply tape bunches of green Easter grass inside the open end of an orange plastic playground cone.

After helping your little ones dramatize the story a few times, make the props available in your dramatic-play area for further storytelling.

Is That a Carrot Under There?

After reading *The Carrot Seed,* your little ones know that the familiar orange part of the carrot grows underground and that the carrot's green leaves are what appear when the carrot sprouts. Invite your budding plant scientists to practice their observation and discrimination skills with this activity. To prepare, fill a large, deep tub with sand. Purchase a few fresh carrots and turnips (with greens attached) and place them near the tub. Have one pair of students at a time visit the center to examine the vegetables. Ask one child to close her eyes while her partner buries the vegetables in the sand so that only the greens are visible. Then have the child open her eyes and try to pick the carrots, identifying them by their leaves. Continue by having the partners switch roles.

Rhyme Time

Gather youngsters around your flannelboard for some carrot poetry! Duplicate the carrots and the rabbit pattern on page 153. (You need more than one copy of the carrots.) Then prepare the pieces for use on your flannelboard. Recite the rhyme shown, placing the pieces on the board as indicated. Then leave the pieces and the flannelboard available for your little ones to use as they recite the poem on their own at center time.

What does a bunny like to munch, munch, munch?   *Put bunny on board.*
A tasty orange carrot he can crunch, crunch, crunch!   *Put one carrot on board.*
He eats one for breakfast; he eats one for lunch—   *Add two more carrots.*
He just loves to eat a whole bunch, bunch, bunch!   *Continue adding carrots.*

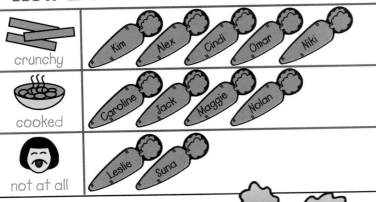

How Do You Like Your Carrots?	
crunchy	Kim Alex Cindi Omar Niki
cooked	Caroline Jack Maggie Nolan
not at all	Leslie Sana

Crunchy or Cooked?

Encourage your little bunnies to nibble some carrots and then cast their votes in this activity, which combines a taste test with a math lesson. To prepare, use the carrot patterns on page 153 to make an orange construction paper carrot for each child. Cut out the carrots and label each one with a child's name. Then create a bar graph similar to the one shown. Also purchase or ask parents to donate a bag of prepared shredded carrots and a large can of carrot slices.

Invite each child to sample a few carrot shreds and a few cooked carrot slices; then have him tape his personalized carrot on the graph to show his preference. Does he like his carrots raw or cooked? Or not at all? Once everyone has voted, count up the carrots in each column and compare the totals.

Carrot Dough

This carrot dough is as good as gold! To make a batch, follow your favorite recipe for basic play dough and mix in shredded carrots and enough powdered tempera paint to give the dough a bright orange color. Set the dough at your play dough center and invite students to use it to make a crop of play dough carrots. Or divide the dough so that each child will have a small portion. Shape each portion into a carrot shape. Wrap it in clear plastic wrap; then tie green curling ribbon around the top. Present each child with his own batch of carrot dough to take home for play!

Kristen Curran—Pre-K, Caring Bear Nursery School & Day Care Inc., Hamden, CT

Bunny, Bunny, Where's Your Carrot?

Hop to it and play a game of Bunny, Bunny, Where's Your Carrot?, played similarly to Doggie, Doggie, Where's Your Bone? To prepare, make a simple bunny-ear headband from pink and white construction paper. Invite one child to wear the headband and sit in a chair. Seat the other children on the floor in a circle around the chair. Then place a carrot beneath the chair.

To play, have the bunny close her eyes; then tap one child in the circle. The tapped child then quietly moves to the chair and takes the carrot. He returns to his seat in the circle and hides the carrot behind his back. Everyone chants, "Bunny, Bunny, who took your carrot?" Then the bunny opens her eyes and tries to guess who took the carrot. Give the child clues, if necessary, until the thief is revealed. The carrot thief then becomes the bunny for the next round of play.

Pam Crane

Carrot-Print Bunnies

Your preschoolers will be all ears when you tell them about this seasonal art project! To prepare, make a simple outline of a bunny face and ears (as shown) on a sheet of white construction paper for each child. Cut a few raw carrots in half lengthwise and a few in half crosswise. Pour some orange tempera paint into shallow trays.

Begin by giving each child in a small group a sheet of copy paper and inviting him to practice making carrot prints, both long ones and circular ones. Then demonstrate how to make a carrot-print bunny. Use a carrot cut lengthwise to make a print on each ear of a prepared bunny face; then use a carrot cut crosswise to make round eyes, a nose, and a mouth. Finish the bunny by using a crayon to add whiskers. Encourage each youngster to make his own carrot-print bunny. Display the finished projects on a bulletin board or classroom wall. "Orange" you glad it's spring?

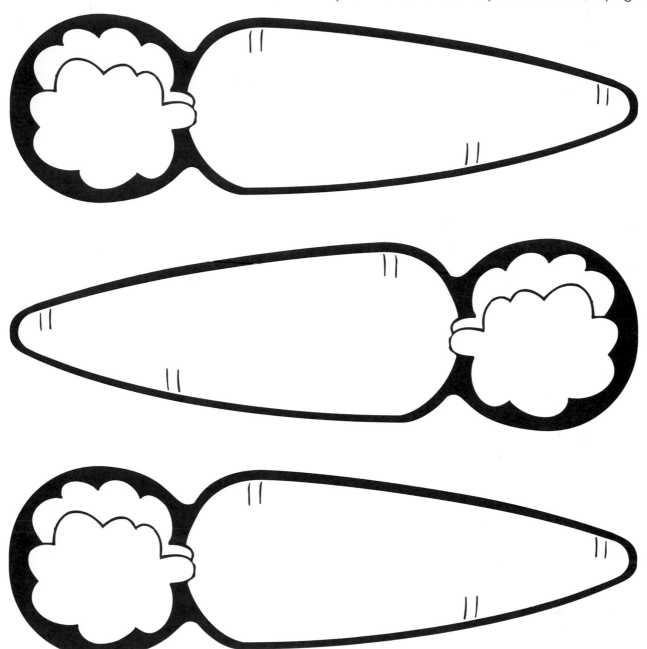

Rabbit Pattern
Use with "Rhyme Time" on page 151.

Red, White, and Blue Gala

Star-Spangled Learning Centers

Celebrations don't have to stop after the Fourth of July! Continue the fun of the holiday by setting up these star-spangled centers using red, white, and blue materials and leftover holiday supplies.

by Michele Stoffel Menzel

Catch the Spirit!

Get set for your celebration by making a class supply of the note on page 159 on red, white, or blue construction paper. Invite students to add patriotic punch to the notes by decorating them with foil star stickers, patriotic stickers, or glitter. Then, just prior to the Fourth of July, send home each child's note to announce your learning center celebration; request that parents donate their leftover holiday supplies; and suggest that students wear red, white, and blue clothing on the days you have your patriotic centers in place.

Patriotic Pizzazz

When the leftover party items you've requested arrive, turn your room into a celebration station by starting with the decor. Have your children help you decorate the room by hanging streamers from the doorway, mounting metallic star-shaped garland at children's eye level, placing holiday-themed tablecloths on the tables, or mounting small flags at each center. Even invite children to paint stars on classroom windows using paint to which a small amount of soap has been added. Look around…a festive flair is in the air!

Star-Spangled Style

If you sent home the note on page 159 announcing your events, then you will have already suggested that the children wear red, white, or blue clothing during the days you have your patriotic centers in place. To make sure that each child has a patriotic item to wear, have her paint a bandana or a kerchief. To prepare, cut a class supply of white fabric squares the size of handkerchiefs. To decorate her square, a child spreads red, blue, or silver glitter fabric paint onto a star-shaped sponge, then presses the sponge onto the square. She continues using different sponges and colors of paint. Once the paint dries, help each child tie on her fabric to form a bandana or a kerchief. How's that for star-spangled style?

Listening Center
Wanted: Star Seekers!

Youngsters' size- and color-recognition skills are sure to shine when they participate in this movement activity. Teach children the song below; then record them singing it several times—each time substituting different color words (*red, white,* or *blue*) and size words (*big* or *small*). Place the tape in your listening center. Then create a path of laminated red, white, and blue construction paper stars in varying sizes. As children visit this center, invite them to play the tape while they jump along the path and pick up stars.

(*sung to the tune of "Pick a Bale of Cotton"*)
Gonna jump down, turn around,
Pick a **big, red** star;
Jump down, turn around,
Pick a star today.

Oh, stars!
Pick a **big, red** star.
Oh, stars!
Pick a star today!

Fine-Motor Center
"Spark-tacular" Sculptures

If you have little ones who tune in to learning through touch, then try this colorful dough activity. Use your favorite recipe to prepare a batch each of uncolored dough, red dough, and blue dough to which silver glitter has been added. When a child visits the center, give her a small ball of each color of dough. Invite her to knead the dough together so that the colors begin to mix; then encourage her to mold her dough into a colorful sculpture. If desired, add star-shaped cookie cutters to the center for more "spark-tacular" fun!

Outdoor Center
Hip, Hip, Hooray! It's a Sidewalk Parade!

Everyone loves a parade! So take a small group outside to a blacktop on the playground or to a sidewalk. Also take a supply of sidewalk chalk in patriotic colors, and provide marching music. Using the chalk, outline a parade path; then have children work together to decorate the path with stars, flags, and fireworks. Invite children to form a line at the beginning of the route and then have them march to the music. Direct the children to take turns leading each other along the route. Hip, hip, hooray!

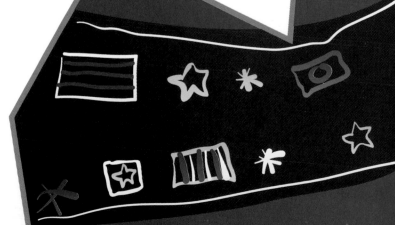

Dramatic-Play Center
Happy Birthday, America!

Your little ones might not fully understand that the Fourth of July is America's birthday, but they are sure to know that every birthday calls for a party! Here's a great center idea that makes use of the party supplies that parents donated, such as holiday-themed paper plates, tablecloths, napkins, cups, plastic utensils, party favors, and confetti. Place all of these items in your dramatic-play area; then let children prepare for birthday celebrations over and over! As they do, they'll have the opportunity to practice sorting, matching, counting, and one-to-one correspondence. The chance to practice these skills is a real reason to celebrate!

Sensory Table
Sparkling Stars and Things

This idea is so simple, yet it provides tons of patriotic fun! Simply add patriotic-themed party confetti to your sand and water tables along with sieves and slotted spoons. Invite little ones to stir, scoop, and sift. As children find the confetti, encourage them to sort, count, and pattern the pieces into red, white, and blue plastic bowls. What a great day for patriotic play!

Art Center
Oh My Stars!

Invite youngsters to add to the red, white, and blue decor by making these star-spangled banners. For each child, use masking tape to create star shapes on a piece of fingerpainting paper. Have each child paint his entire sheet with any combination of red and blue paint. Then, when the paint dries, assist each child as he carefully removes the tape. Oh my, I spy stars!

Science Center
Fireworks Display

This see-and-touch discovery center invites little ones to watch changes in the shape, color, and texture of frozen paints *and* to create paintings that explode with color! Prepare for this discovery by layering each section of a well-cleaned foam egg carton with red, white, and blue BioColor paint (available from Discount School Supply, 1-800-627-2829). Firmly close the lid; then insert a separate craft stick through the lid and into each section of the carton. When the paint is frozen, take the carton out of the freezer and let it sit for just a few minutes. Put some of the individual sticks of paint in the center for children to use and observe; then put the carton back in the freezer.

Encourage children to use the frozen paints to draw on white construction paper. Then, as the paint melts, have each child paint a design beside her original drawing. When the paint melts completely, encourage her to fingerpaint. Mount the paintings together for an explosion of color.

Math Center
Starstruck

Math is marvelous when youngsters use colorful stars to create patterns. Cut red, white, and blue stars from craft foam to stock your math center. Have a child use two different colors of stars to form a pattern, such as *white star, blue star, white star, blue star*. Next, have her chant the pattern she sees. Encourage her to continue forming simple patterns in which each color of star is repeated one time. After children have completed the center, reward them with foil star stickers. Wow!

Math Center
Stars and Stripes Patterning

Patterning practice is easy when children create a path of stars and stripes! Cut at least ten each of red, white, and blue streamer lengths and ten each of red, white, and blue construction paper stars. Put the items in your math center. When a child visits the center, help him create a pattern using the stars and stripes (streamers). For example, his pattern might be *red star, blue stripe, red star, blue stripe*. To reinforce the pattern, clap a steady beat as the child walks along his path. Yeah! He's got the beat!

Cooking Center
Striped Ice

Looking for an easy way to help your little ones beat the heat? Then try these shivery treats as a cool addition to your tricolored celebration. In preparation, place a plastic bowl full of crushed ice; an ice-cream scoop; two squeeze bottles, one containing red juice and the other containing blue juice; and a class supply of clear plastic cups and flexible drinking straws in your cooking center.

To make a striped ice treat, a child fills his cup with one scoop of ice and then drizzles red juice and blue juice over the ice. Next, he places a straw in the ice and enjoys his slushy treat! Wow! Cool stripes!

Fine-Motor Center
Squishy Star Swirls

Give youngsters' fingers a workout with this shaving cream twist! To make one star swirl bag, use a black permanent marker to draw a few star-shaped outlines onto a large resealable, plastic freezer bag. Squirt a few dollops of white shaving cream along with either red or blue food coloring or tempera paint into the bag. If desired, add a sprinkle of glitter. Reinforce the seal of the bag with clear packing tape. Place several of the bags in a fine-motor center. Invite children at the center to explore the bags by squishing them and tracing the star outlines with their fingers. Ooh, squishy swirl fun!

Block Center
Building Blocks for Two

This patriotic partnering activity will encourage children to sort, count, and compare red, white, and blue blocks while also fostering creativity. Use red, white, or blue tape to create two large stars on the floor of your block area. (Make sure the stars are big enough for a child to build structures inside.) Put a matching set of DUPLO blocks in each center so that the two sets correspond in the number of each color of blocks.

Invite a pair of children to visit the block center. Help them sort the blocks by color and then compare their sets to see that they have the same number of each color. Then encourage each child to use her set of blocks to build a structure within her star shape. Help the partners realize that even though they have the same materials, they can use their creativity to build different structures. If desired, have children top off their structures with miniature American flags.

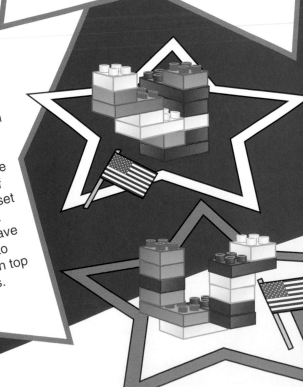

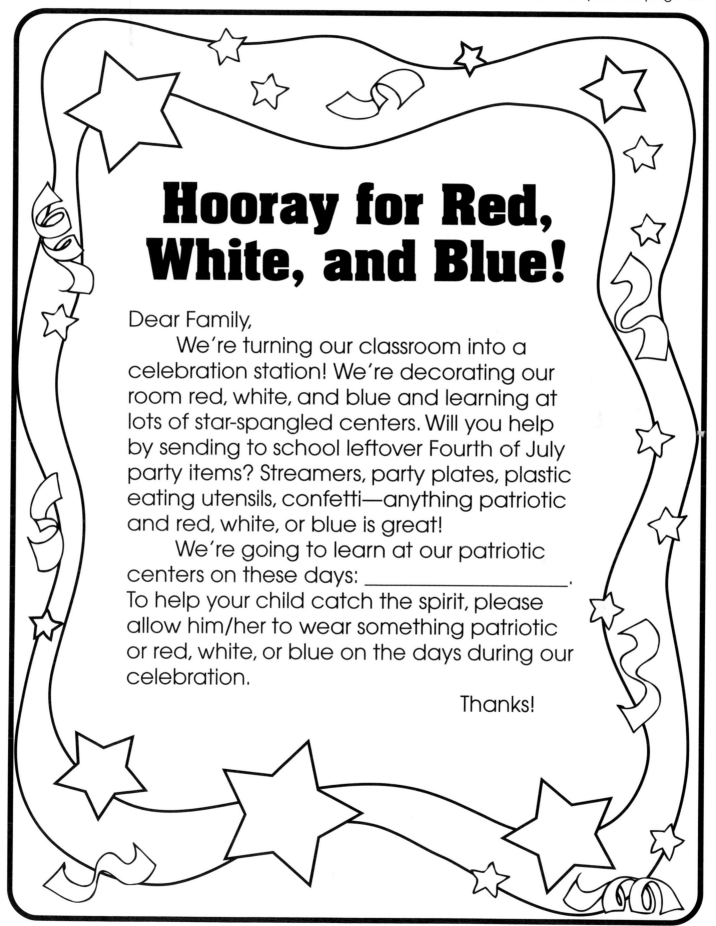

Hooray for Red, White, and Blue!

Dear Family,

We're turning our classroom into a celebration station! We're decorating our room red, white, and blue and learning at lots of star-spangled centers. Will you help by sending to school leftover Fourth of July party items? Streamers, party plates, plastic eating utensils, confetti—anything patriotic and red, white, or blue is great!

We're going to learn at our patriotic centers on these days: _____. To help your child catch the spirit, please allow him/her to wear something patriotic or red, white, or blue on the days during our celebration.

Thanks!

Backyard Barbecue

Hear the sizzle? That's the sound of excitement as your youngsters get all fired up about these centers with a backyard barbecue theme! So put on your apron and grab your spatula—it's time for a cookout!

by Ada Goren

Dramatic-Play Area
Get Grillin'

Sure, it's fun to pretend to cook inside, but how about pretending to cook outside? Transform your housekeeping area into a backyard ready for a summer feast. Bring in a child's picnic table and benches. Create a grill by arranging brick blocks into a square and then placing an oven rack on top. Provide props such as aprons, oven mitts, barbecue tools, paper plates, plastic utensils and cups, and plastic serving pieces. Cut hamburgers, hot dogs, buns, and toppings from colorful craft foam and sponges. Store the pieces in plastic food containers with lids. Choose some pretend foods from your collection that will be appropriate for this play theme, such as corn on the cob and potatoes. Then invite little ones to come on over to flip some burgers and chow down!

Game Center
Barbecue Lotto

The object of this game is to fill your plate with a tasty menu of barbecue treats! To prepare, make several copies of the barbecue food pictures on page 164. Color the foods as desired; then cut them out. Make lotto boards by gluing various combinations of foods onto paper plates. For example, one plate might have a hot dog, corn on the cob, watermelon, and pie, while another has a hamburger, chips, lemonade, and a Popsicle treat. Make as many plates as you wish to have players. Put the remaining cards in a stack. To play, each child takes a plate. He then draws food cards from the stack, trying to match the foods on his plate. The first player to complete his menu is the winner.

Art Center
Give 'em a Squeeze

What makes a hamburger or a hot dog extra yummy? The ketchup and mustard, of course! Spread some fun to your art center by inviting youngsters to paint with ketchup and mustard—or, actually, red and yellow paint in condiment squeeze bottles! Purchase plastic ketchup and mustard bottles; then partially fill them with slightly thinned red and yellow tempera paint. Set out large sheets of paper and let the squeezing and squirting begin! Or, for more fun, use a black marker to draw simple hot dog and hamburger shapes on the painting paper. After the paint dries, cut out these giant barbecue delights and put them on your classroom walls for a delicious display!

Blocks Area
Cooler Capacity

No backyard barbecue would be complete without some ice-cold drinks to accompany the food. So bring out the coolers and have youngsters fill them with blocks of "ice" and bottles of soda. Put three different sizes of coolers in your blocks area. Collect a supply of clean, empty soda bottles in various sizes, too. For ice, use small square wooden blocks or colorful wooden cubes. Ask your preschoolers to experiment: Which cooler will hold the most ice? The most bottles? The largest bottles? Visit this center to encourage youngsters to try various combinations and to model math vocabulary, such as *more, less, most, least, fewest, small, medium,* and *large.*

Math Center
Seeds on Slices

A slice of juicy watermelon just might be the highlight of a summer cookout. So set up this watermelon seed counting center complete with real seeds! To prepare, make ten copies of the watermelon slice pattern on page 165. Color the patterns; then add a numeral from 1 to 10 on each slice. Cut out the slices and laminate them for durability. Collect a large supply of real watermelon seeds, rinsing and drying the seeds thoroughly. (If desired, save the seeds when preparing Watermelon Smoothies below.) Make 10 seed pouches by placing 1–10 seeds in a snack-size zippered plastic bag. Reinforce each seal with tape. Invite each child to spread the slices on the floor or on a tabletop and then place the corresponding bag of seeds on each slice. For an added challenge, encourage the child to arrange the slices in numerical order before placing the seeds on them.

Snack Center
Watermelon Smoothies

Gather your youngsters in small groups to whip up these creamy watermelon delights! Little ones can help discard the watermelon seeds, squeeze the lime juice, and measure the yogurt and ice cubes.

Watermelon Smoothies
(serves 6)

3 c. watermelon chunks, seeds removed
juice of 1 lime
1 c. vanilla yogurt
1 c. ice cubes

Put all ingredients in a blender and process until smooth. Pour into cups and sip with straws.

Manipulatives Center
Forks, Knives, and Spoons

Expecting a big crowd for your barbecue? Better see how many plastic utensils you have on hand! Encourage your little ones to count and compare plastic forks, knives, and spoons with this activity. To prepare, purchase (or ask parents to donate) a supply of plastic utensils. Place varying numbers of the three types of utensils in a basket. Then have younger preschoolers sort the utensils into three groups by type. For older preschoolers, create a simple graph on a length of bulletin board paper (as shown). In a small group, ask the children to sort the forks, knives, and spoons onto the graph. Then count the total of each type of utensil and discuss what the graph reveals.

Literacy Center
Serving Up the Alphabet

Any barbecue planner knows you can never have enough paper plates! Use a few to serve up some alphabet practice for your older preschoolers! To prepare, gather 26 small white paper plates. Print a different letter of the alphabet on each plate. Place the stack of plates (with the letters in random order) near your classroom alphabet strip or provide a small alphabet strip at your literacy center. Ask a child to lay the plates out on the floor in alphabetical order, using the alphabet strip as a guide. Easy as A, B, C!

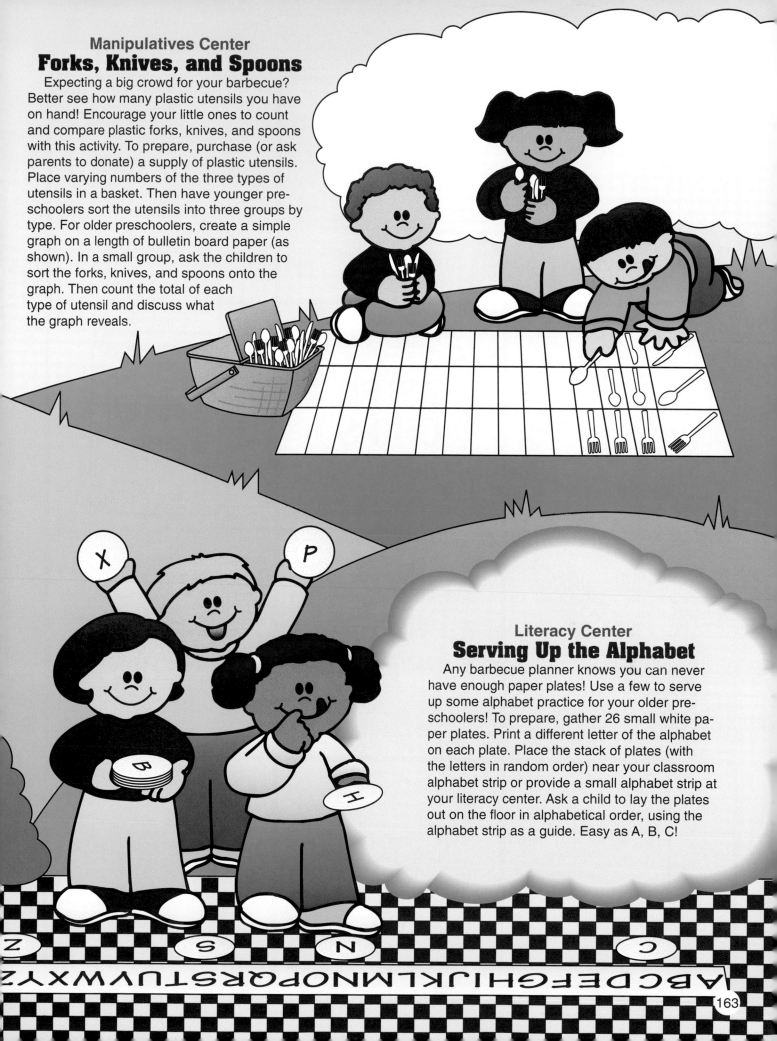

Barbecue Foods

Use with "Barbecue Lotto" on page 160.

©The Education Center, Inc. • *The Best of* The Mailbox® • *Preschool* • TEC60784

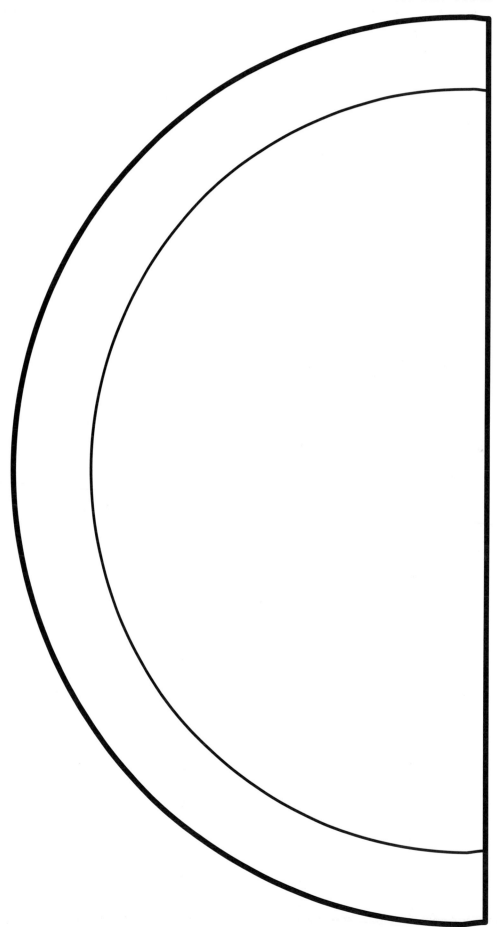

Slides, Swings, and Playground Things!

Step outside for some unique learning opportunities with these pleasing playground ideas!

Around!

Down!

Under!

Going Down!

You've most likely painted with a marble in a pan. Now paint with a ball on the slide! To prepare, line the board of a slide with a strip of white bulletin board paper. Set a shallow pan of paint at the top of the slide and a box at the bottom to catch the ball. Stand behind a child as he climbs to the top of the slide; then provide him with a large spoon and a ball. Direct the child to roll the ball in the paint. Then have him use the spoon to scoop out the ball and roll it down the slide. Have each child repeat the activity using different types of balls and colors of paint. Look out below! *art exploration, fine-motor skills*

Cassie Campbell—Preschool
Burrier Child Development Center, Richmond, KY

Positions, Positions

Set up an outdoor obstacle course, and learning positional words and spatial terms will be a breeze! In advance, create a short course that will have students in different positions. For example, have students walk *around* your play structure, run *under* the bridge, and then slide *down* the slide. Invite a small group of children to the course and encourage each child to say the appropriate positional word as she moves through each obstacle. "Around, under, down!" *positional words, gross-motor skills, following directions*

Karen Almond
Royston Elementary School, Royston, GA

Fancy Fence

If there is a chain-link fence around your playground, dress it up with this weaving activity! In advance, purchase remnants of colorful double-knit polyester fabric and then cut the fabric into strips. Tie one end of each strip to a different link on the fence. Then invite your youngsters to weave the strips through the links. The weaving will add a splash of color to the fence, and, best of all, the polyester fabric will weather the outdoor elements. To freshen up strips that have become soiled, simply toss them into the washing machine. Ah, the beauty of polyester! *fine-motor skills*

Betsy Fuhrmann—Pre-K
Dodds School, Springfield, IL

This Looks Familiar!

Just how well do your students know the playground? Find out with this idea! In advance, take close-up photographs of small details on your playground, such as a logo on a piece of equipment, the seat of a swing, or a knob on a water fountain. (For best results, use a camera that will take clear pictures at close range.) Provide each child in a small group with a different photograph; then direct the child to find the item in the photo. If necessary, help the child narrow his search by giving him a clue about the item. "You use this when you are thirsty…." *critical thinking, visual discrimination*

Painting Practice

Invite youngsters to give your playground a fresh coat of pretend paint. In advance, visit a local paint store and request donations of small, clean, empty paint cans. Fill each can with water and place a large paintbrush in the can. Be sure the can is still light enough for a child to carry. Invite your youngsters to take a can and a brush and paint the playground. Watch out! This paint is really wet! *dramatic play*

167

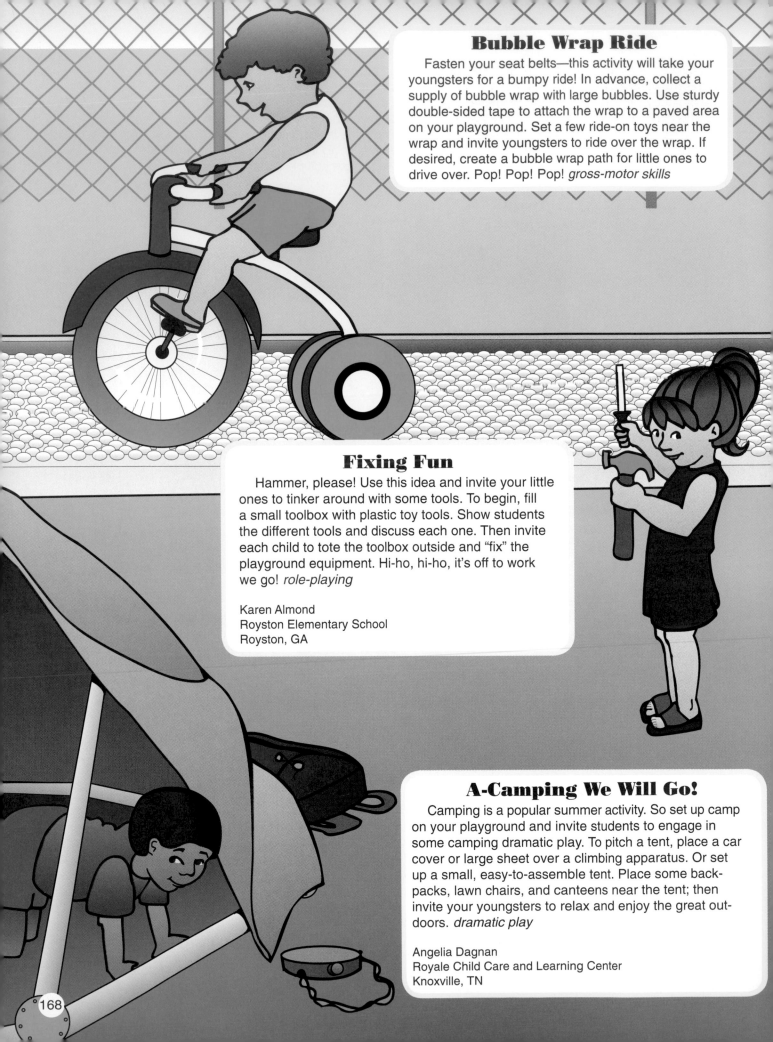

Bubble Wrap Ride

Fasten your seat belts—this activity will take your youngsters for a bumpy ride! In advance, collect a supply of bubble wrap with large bubbles. Use sturdy double-sided tape to attach the wrap to a paved area on your playground. Set a few ride-on toys near the wrap and invite youngsters to ride over the wrap. If desired, create a bubble wrap path for little ones to drive over. Pop! Pop! Pop! *gross-motor skills*

Fixing Fun

Hammer, please! Use this idea and invite your little ones to tinker around with some tools. To begin, fill a small toolbox with plastic toy tools. Show students the different tools and discuss each one. Then invite each child to tote the toolbox outside and "fix" the playground equipment. Hi-ho, hi-ho, it's off to work we go! *role-playing*

Karen Almond
Royston Elementary School
Royston, GA

A-Camping We Will Go!

Camping is a popular summer activity. So set up camp on your playground and invite students to engage in some camping dramatic play. To pitch a tent, place a car cover or large sheet over a climbing apparatus. Or set up a small, easy-to-assemble tent. Place some backpacks, lawn chairs, and canteens near the tent; then invite your youngsters to relax and enjoy the great outdoors. *dramatic play*

Angelia Dagnan
Royale Child Care and Learning Center
Knoxville, TN

Swing Song

Stimulate the musical side of your youngsters with this swinging idea! Thread short lengths of twine or sturdy yarn through several large jingle bells; then tie the bells to the links on the swings' chains. As your little ones begin swinging, the bells will begin ringing! That's music to my ears! *auditory stimulation*

Sandy Designs

Oh, the nifty designs your youngsters will create with this outdoor process-art activity! In advance, gather the materials listed. Thread the length of yarn through the spring in the clothespin and tie the ends together. Then head outside with your youngsters and follow the directions below. *art exploration*

Materials needed:
resealable plastic bag per child
spring-type clothespin
24" length of yarn
white Con-Tact paper
clear Con-Tact paper
spoon
scissors (for teacher use only)
colored sand

Step 1: Have a child place one or two spoonfuls of colored sand in a resealable plastic bag.

Step 2: Seal the bag and then clip the clothespin to it as shown.

Step 3: Place a sheet of Con-Tact paper on the ground, adhesive side up.

Step 4: Have the child grasp the yarn and hold the bag over the Con-Tact paper.

Step 5: Cut a small hole in the bottom corner of the bag so the sand slowly trickles out.

Step 6: Direct the child to gently swing the bag over the paper to create a design with the sand.

Step 7: Shake off any excess sand from the paper; then cover it with a sheet of clear Con-Tact paper.

Bull's-Eye!

Here's an eye-hand coordination activity that's right on target for preschoolers. In advance, duplicate the pattern on page 171. Use a red marker to color the center of the pattern and then laminate it. Mount the pattern at children's level on a wall or pole on your playground. Fill a few empty squirt bottles with water and set them a short distance away from the target. Invite each child to pull open the top of a bottle, aim it toward the target, and then squeeze the bottle so that the water streams out toward the bull's-eye. For added incentive, make a supply of patterns and paint the centers with red watercolor paint. When a child hits the bull's-eye with water, the paint will begin to run. *eye-hand coordination*

Clean Up!

Any way you toss it, this game will be a winner with your youngsters. Find a large open area on your playground. Use a rope to divide the area into two equal sections; then place several balls in each section. Divide your class into two teams and have each team stand in a different section. Begin the game by shouting, "Clean the playground!" Then have each team try to "clean" its section by throwing all of the balls into the other team's section. After a minute or two, shout, "Stop cleaning!" and have each team count the number of balls, if any, in its area. *gross-motor skills, counting*

Sandra Faulkner—Four-Year-Olds
Kernersville Moravian Preschool
Winston-Salem, NC

170

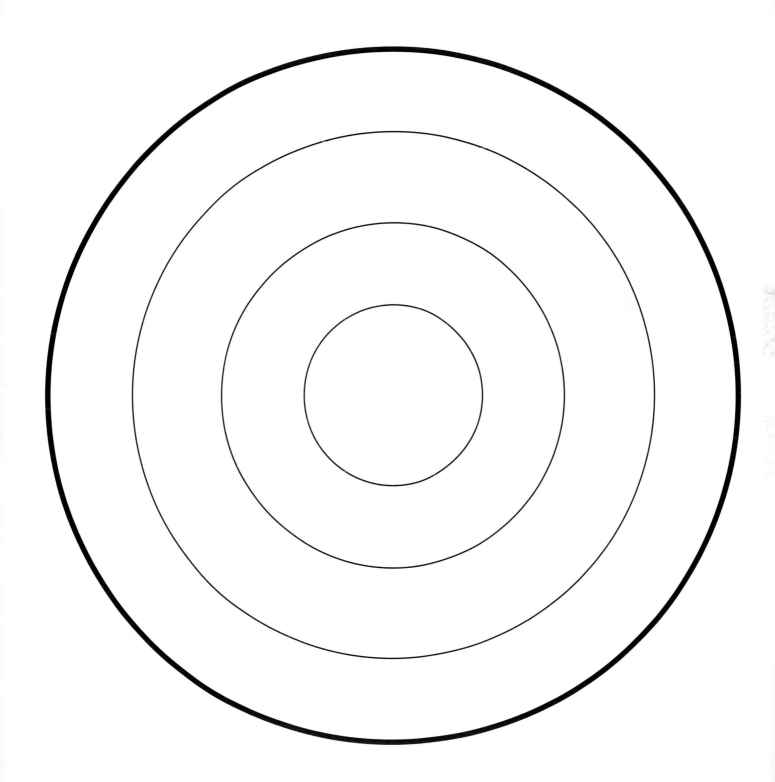

See You Later, Alligator!

Use these end-of-the-year ideas to wind down
your school year with an all-out alligator celebration!

ideas contributed by Lucia Kemp Henry

An Alligator a Day

Count down the last five days of school with this idea.
In advance, plan at least one alligator activity for each
of the last five days of school. Cut out five construction
paper alligators. Write the numeral 5 on one alligator; then
flip it over and write the alligator activity planned for the
first day of the countdown. Program the next alligator with
the numeral 4 and the activity planned for the *second* day
of the countdown. Program the remaining alligators in a
similar manner so that each one is labeled with a different
activity and number from 1 to 5. Use pushpins to mount
the alligators in a display similar to the one shown.

During circle time invite your youngsters to chant,
"How many days are left in school? Let's count the
alligators in the pool!" Have students count the alligators
on the display and then say how many days remain. Invite
a child to find the alligator with that number and remove
it from the display. Then read aloud the activity written on
the back of the alligator. Five, four, three, two, one. The
alligator countdown has begun!

How Many Days Are Left in School?

1 2
3 4

Learn an alligator goodbye song.

An Alligator Goodbye

During the last week of school, have your youngsters
sing the following song at the end of each day. On the
final day of school, sing the song one last time and
then wish your little ones a wonderful summer. Singing
a familiar song sure makes saying goodbye easier!

(sung to the tune of "Glory, Glory Hallelujah")

See you later, alligator!
See you later, alligator!
See you later, alligator!
It's time to say goodbye.

Preschool Memories

This alligator display shows off youngsters' creativity and fondest preschool memories. To make one alligator painting, drop a spoonful of green fingerpaint on a sheet of paper and then sprinkle some sand onto the paint. Invite a child to mix the sand into the paint and create a textured fingerpainting. When the paint is dry, cut out an alligator shape from the paper. Have the child stick on a hole reinforcer eye and white construction paper teeth. Invite the child to describe a favorite school memory. Write her response on a white paper speech bubble. Mount each child's alligator and speech bubble on a bulletin board titled "See You Later, Alligator." Now doesn't this gator gathering make a great farewell display?

I liked it when we took a field trip to the zoo.
Tameka

Alligator Applause

Need a way to thank your classroom volunteers, student teachers, or other special helpers? Give them a little alligator applause with this thank-you poster! To make one, cut a 3' x 3' square from blue bulletin board paper. Use a permanent marker to write a message in the center of the paper. Next, invite each child to make a green handprint on the edge of the poster; then write her name near the print. When the paint is dry, have the child draw an eye and add paper teeth on the print. Carefully roll up the poster, tie a ribbon around it, and then present it to a special someone!

Ben Tyler Sammy

Miss Cox, Thanks for helping in our classroom!

Suna Jackson

See you later, Alligator!

Ashley Cassie

Michael Jamie Tameka

Say Goodbye With a Grin

When it's time to say goodbye, give each child a smile with this photo-card idea. In advance, have an adult volunteer take a photograph of you with each child. Then have the film developed into 3½" x 5" prints.

To make one card, copy the patterns on page 175 onto green construction paper. Cut out the patterns; then staple the cover to the card along the left side. Next, glue a photograph of you and a child onto the back of the cover. Write the child's name on the line. Sign the card and then glue a small wiggle eye sticker onto the alligator. Goodbye, little gator!

Thanks for a great year, Sammy!

Love, Mrs. Henry

173

Presenting Preschool Alligators

If you're planning an end-of-the-year program, use the following alligator-themed ideas to add a little *snap* to your presentation!

Gator Gear

Get each child geared up for the program with this nifty alligator hat. To make one, duplicate page 176 onto green construction paper; then cut out each pattern. Next, read through the directions shown. Gather the necessary materials and then help the child follow the steps to complete his alligator headgear. During the program, have your students wear their hats as they perform "All the Preschool Alligators" below.

Step 1: Make tabs on the snout pattern by cutting along the dotted lines.

Step 2: Bend the tabs up and staple them to a headband. Then fold down each side of the snout along the lines.

Step 3: Glue a white paper circle to each eye; then glue the eyes onto the headband.

Step 4: Glue a paper eye onto each circle. Glue white paper teeth onto the snout.

Lights, Camera, Action!

Put your preschoolers in the spotlight with an alligator poem that shows what they know! Prior to your presentation, have your little ones practice the actions as you recite the poem below. When you're ready to perform, have each child don her alligator hat (see "Gator Gear"). Then recite the poem as your little alligators act it out.

All the Preschool Alligators

All the preschool alligators
Stand here in a row.
Our gators want to show you
All the things they know!

These gators know their numbers.
They know some letters, too.
These gators know a nursery rhyme.
They'll say it now for you.

These gators can say, "Thank you."
These gators can say, "Please."
These gators say, "Excuse me!"
Every time they sneeze!

These gators like to read.
These gators run and play.
These gators want to say goodbye
The alligator way!

Stand in a row facing audience.

Bow to audience.

Count to ten.
Say, "A, B, C."

Recite a nursery rhyme.

Say, "Thank you."
Say, "Please."

Pretend to sneeze and then say, "Excuse me!"

Pretend to open and read a book.
Run in place.

Wave and say, "See you later, alligator!"
Then clap hands together and say, "Snap!"

174

cover

See You Later, Alligator

©The Education Center, Inc.

card

Thanks for a great year,

_____!

Love, _____

Alligator Hat Patterns
Use with "Gator Gear" on page 174.

snout

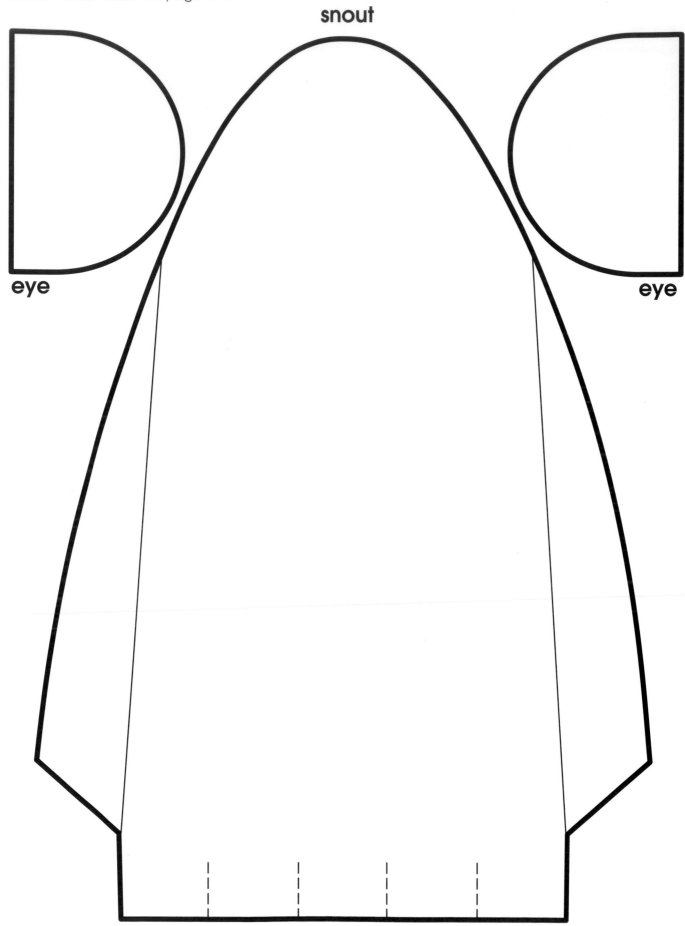

eye

eye

Special Features

Get Spotted at the Library!

A Family Night Event

If you're looking for a fun family event, then these ideas for a night at the library are sure to hit the spot! You'll find a note to send to parents and planning tips for a fun evening together. Soon everyone will want to get spotted at the library!

ideas by LeeAnn Collins—Director, Sunshine Preschool, Lansing, MI

There's a Spot for You at the Library

Parents are sure to "paws" to read this unique note! To announce your family night at the library, write a note similar to the one shown containing the date and time of your event. Duplicate the note and the dog pattern on page 180 to create a class supply; then cut them out. Have each child color the spots on a dog pattern if desired. Cut along the bold lines of each dog's mouth; then slip a note into each slit, taping it to the back of the dog to secure it. Send the notes home to let all the families know they are invited to the event!

Books in the Spotlight

Here's another way to promote your family night at the library. First, read (or paraphrase) the following books during storytime. Then send home each of these library books with each child, in turn, to read and return the next day. Attach a note to each book reminding parents of the date and time of the event.

There's a spot for your family at the library!

Please join us for family night at the library! A storytime, a library hunt, and a time to check out books are included in the fun. We'll also take a photo of every family spotted at the library.

Meet us at South Branch Library located at 500 Weaver St. on Monday, Sept. 18 at 6:30 P.M.

Don't forget! Our family night at the library is September 18 at 6:30 P.M. To get ready for the event, you might want to read this book (or discuss the pictures) with your child. Happy reading!

I Took My Frog to the Library
Written by Eric A. Kimmel

A Visit to the Sesame Street Library
Written by Deborah Hautzig

I Like Books
Written and illustrated by Anthony Browne

I Like the Library
Written and illustrated by Anne Rockwell

My Hometown Library
Written by William Jaspersohn

Library Spot Check

Before your family night, visit the library to meet with the librarian who will help you coordinate the events of the evening. Here are some questions you might ask:

- Is a snack an option for your family night at the library?
- What are the requirements for an adult or child applying for a library card? (If a form must be completed to apply for a card, get copies to send home to families in advance.)
- Where can the families meet for a group storytime? Is there a librarian who can lead the storytime?
- Which spots in the library should be featured during the library hunt? (See "What Can You Spot at the Library?")

What Can You Spot at the Library?

Set up a library hunt to make sure parents and children are aware of the many things a library offers. Select five areas of the library that you would like families to visit, such as the computers, audio recordings, picture books, videos, and circulation desk. Label each spot on a copy of the dog pattern (page 180) with a different area. Duplicate the pattern to make a class supply. Just prior to the event, designate each of these areas in the library with a labeled, large poster board circle. Also place a set of matching dot stickers in each area.

When it's time for the hunt, give each family a dog pattern. Challenge each family to visit the designated areas of the library and to attach a dot sticker from each area to the dog pattern. Encourage them to visit the circulation desk last so that they can take home their choice of materials.

Photo Spot

Arrange for a volunteer to stand near the circulation desk or exit to take a picture of each family as that family completes the evening. Later, send each photo home in the same manner the invitation was sent home—tucked into the mouth of the spotted dog pattern (see "There's a Spot for You at the Library" on page 178). The photo is sure to be a reminder that the library is a spot to visit often. Smile and say, "Library!"

computers

videos

audio recordings

circulation desk

picture books

SPOT

179

Pattern

Use with "There's a Spot for You at the Library" on page 178
and "What Can You Spot at the Library?"
and "Photo Spot" on page 179.

SPOT

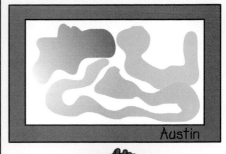

Austin

You're invited to try these helpful hints and easy activities designed to make your open house a surefire success!

Extra Clothes Exhibit

Do you have youngsters bring an extra set of clothing to school in case of an emergency? Use those extra clothes to make a clever display of student work! Stuff each set of clothing with newspaper; then display the clothing on a wall or bulletin board. Help each child create a paper plate face with yarn hair to complete the preschooler look-alike. Then display each child's artwork above and below his stuffed likeness. If desired, overlap the sleeves on each child's shirt and use a clothespin to attach a photograph of the actual child so that it looks as though the stuffed likeness is holding the photo.

For added fun, stuff a set of your own clothing and make a paper plate likeness of yourself. Position this substitute teacher so it's sitting in your chair or standing in the front of the room!

Sue Dupree—Four- and Five-Year-Olds
First Presbyterian Child Development Center
Gainesville, GA

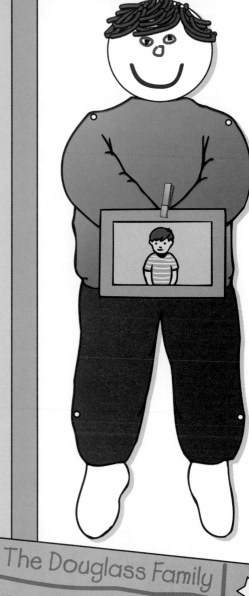

Family Feet

Here's a fun way for families to put their best feet forward at your open house—a family feet collage! In advance, send home with each child a parent note similar to the one shown and two 12" x 18" sheets of construction paper, each in a different color. Mount each family's fancy footwork on a display for open house. And, of course, this display would not be complete if it were missing the teacher's feet! Be sure to add your own collage to the display!

Nancy M. Lotzer—PreK
The Hillcrest Academy
Dallas, TX

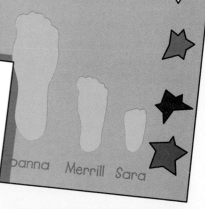

The Douglass Family

Danna   Merrill   Sara

Dear Parents,

We are decorating our classroom and need a hand—and some feet! Please help your child complete this "Family Feet" project and return it to school. Attached you will find two pieces of construction paper. Choose one and trace each family member's foot onto it. Help your child cut out each foot and then glue it onto the remaining sheet of paper. Write your family's name on the top of the paper. Decorate the paper and then return it by Monday, September 17. Thank you for your help!

Lights, Camera...Action!

Open house is all about educating families about their children's school experiences, so why not show them firsthand? Throughout the first few weeks of school, videotape some of your classroom routines, some of the students' favorite activities, and some free play at your classroom centers. Review the tape before open house to be sure you've included every child in your group. During open house, play the tape without sound and narrate the activities that parents are watching.

Carolyn Fleet—Three- and Four-Year-Olds
Sandwich Village Preschool and Childcare
Sandwich, MA

Dustin and his mom, Carla, play with blocks.

Theo and his dad, Bill, play with trucks.

Look Who's Been Playing Here!

When parents visit for open house, snap a photo of each of them playing in a center or performing an activity she knows her child enjoys. Have the photos developed; then glue each one to a card labeled with both the parent's and child's names. Mount the cards on a display titled "Look Who's Been Playing Here at School!" Your little ones will look to the display for a comforting family reminder and parents can look over the display to learn one another's names!

Nancy Garron—Preschool
Little Angels Christian Preschool
Dover, MA

The Eyes Have It

Challenge your open house visitors to identify their children on a unique display that helps stir up conversation. To prepare, take a photo of each child on the first day of school. Develop the photos; then cover each one with a sheet of construction paper. Cut out a space in the paper to reveal only the child's eyes in the photo beneath it. Then number each covered picture and make a list of the numbers and corresponding children for your reference. Display the covered photos during your open house and invite parents to try to identify their children by looking only at the eyes. Have each parent tell you the number of the photo he believes to be his child. When he has guessed correctly, uncover the photo and give it to him to keep.

Tammy Lutz—Head Start
George E. Greene Elementary
Bad Axe, MI

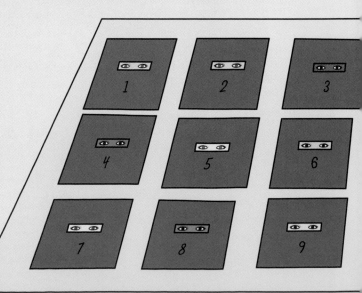

Scavenger Hunt

Send parents on a fun and informative scavenger hunt when they come for open house. Make up a scavenger hunt sheet, listing questions for parents to answer or areas of your room for them to visit and check off. Duplicate the scavenger hunt sheet and pass it out to parents as they arrive. Use the hunt to familiarize parents with your classroom routines, point parents to children's work, and give reminders about supplies that need to be turned in. Don't forget to include an opportunity for them to ask you questions as one of the items on the list!

Kelly Shuffield—PreK
Fulbright Elementary
Little Rock, AR

Scavenger Hunt for Miss Emily's Room

Welcome! Here's a fun game to help you get to know our classroom better! As you look around, check off each item or answer each question. Be sure to bring me your sheet and ask me any questions when you're done!

1) What color is your child's group?
2) Find your child's cubby. Is there an extra change of clothes inside? If not, please send one ASAP!
3) How many days have we been in school? (Hint: Look at our counting display.)
4) Find your child's self-portrait. Each child will draw a new one at the beginning of each month.
5) Can you figure out which centers your child visited this afternoon?
6) Check out our rocket display. Can you find your child's rocket?
7) Come by to ask me questions!

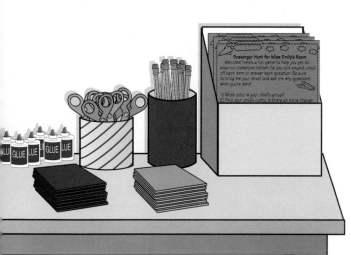

Parent Provisions

If you like to set up a craft activity at your open house, consider providing enough materials so that each child and each parent can make an individual project. With this idea, children *and* parents will be saying, "Look! I made it all by myself!"

Julie Ann Male
Kishwaukee College Even Start
Malta, IL

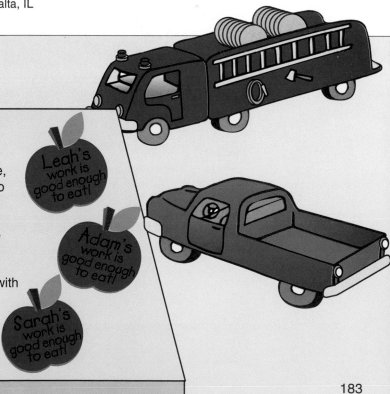

"A-peel-ing" Magnets

These refrigerator magnets make a fun favor for parents to take home after their open house visit. Before open house, work one-on-one with each child to assemble her magnet. To make one, cut an apple shape from red craft foam. Help the child cut out a green craft foam leaf and a brown craft foam stem. Then direct her to glue them onto the apple. When the glue is dry, use a paint pen to program the apple as shown. Then attach a strong self-adhesive magnetic strip onto the back of the apple. You're sure to get a crop of compliments with this idea!

Sarah Booth—Four- and Five-Year-Olds
Messiah Nursery School
South Williamsport, PA

Golden Opportunities

We asked preschool teachers from across the country to share their best transition tips and time fillers. What did we get? A pot of golden learning opportunities that will help you make the most of every minute!

Something Looks the Same

Choose two or three students who have something in common, such as hair color, gender, or an article of clothing. Have them stand in front of the class and then ask your youngsters, "What do these children have in common?"

Barbara F. Backer
Charleston, SC

What's in a Name?

Use a display of student names to reinforce a variety of skills. Give each child, in turn, a direction such as "Find a name that begins with the letter S," "Find a name that has two Es," or "Find a name that has five letters."

Lynn Schmeling—Four-Year-Old Kindergarten
Humboldt Park School
Milwaukee, WI

A New Twist on Pipe Cleaners

Provide each child with a pipe cleaner. Call out a shape and have each child twist the pipe cleaner into that shape.

Rebecca Stevens—Preschool
The Children's Express
Cresson, PA

Storytime Transition

Settle youngsters down for a story with an action rhyme that helps develop motor skills.

Sometimes my hands are at my side.
Sometimes behind my back they hide.
Sometimes my fingers wiggle so.
Wiggle fast.
Wiggle slow.
Sometimes my hands go clap, clap, clap!
But now they're resting in my lap.
They're as quiet as can be
Because it's storytime, you see.

Mary Ann Holmes—Preschool
Christian Life Assembly
Stroudsburg, PA

Math in a Minute

Introduce little ones to addition and subtraction with this tip. Provide each child with five craft sticks; then say a math sentence such as "If you have five sticks and take away two sticks, how many do you have left?" Encourage youngsters to use their sticks to solve the problem.

Marianne Edwards—PreK
Angels Unlimited Preschool
Red Wing, MN

Feelings

Laminate magazine pictures that depict different scenarios, such as a child in need of a bandage, children laughing, or a child standing beside a spill. Show students each picture and invite them to discuss what the person may be feeling. If desired, also have students discuss what they think might have happened.

Heather McDaniel—Four-Year-Olds
Columbine Area Preschool
Littleton, CO

Shaping Up!

Scatter a class supply of construction paper shapes in your circle-time area. (Or use die-cut numbers or letters.) Hold open a gallon-size resealable plastic bag. Name a shape; then direct a child to find that shape and place it in the bag. Continue until each child has had a turn and all of the shapes are in the bag.

Kerstin Afrasiabi—Preschool
Palmdale United Methodist
Palmdale, CA

Classification Game

Give students a topic such as things that are red, things that fly, or things that smell good. Then have your youngsters brainstorm a list of appropriate words.

Heather Miller—PreK

Now Hear This!

If you and your class are outside with a few moments to spare, try this listening activity. Have your youngsters stand quietly and listen to the sounds around them. After a minute or two, invite one child to name a sound that he heard. Then encourage him to mimic the noise. What a great activity for those early days of spring!

Heather Miller—PreK
Creative Play School
Auburn, IN

Ready or Not, Here I Come!

This adaptation of hide-and-seek makes a perfect five-minute filler! Take a full-length photo of each child and then cut the child out of the picture. Place the cutouts inside an envelope and draw one at random. Direct the child in that photo to hide his cutout in your classroom while the other students close their eyes. Then have classmates open their eyes and search for the hidden "child."

Heather Miller—PreK

Snap!
Button!
Z-z-z-i-p!

Looking for a way to help your little ones dress for success? With this collection of ideas, teaching self-help skills will be a snap…and a button…and a zipper!

ideas by Lucia Kemp Henry

Jackets Required

Buttons, zippers, snaps. So many types of fasteners! Help your students sort it all out with this circle-time activity that involves their own jackets and coats. To begin, invite each child to put on his jacket and come to the circle. Discuss why we should keep our coats buttoned, zipped, or snapped in chilly weather. Have each child identify the type of fastener on his jacket; then let the sorting begin! Place three large Hula-Hoop toys on the floor. Or use lengths of yarn to make three large circles. Designate one circle for zippers, one for buttons, and one for snaps. Direct students to sort themselves by fasteners and stand in the appropriate circle. Then count the number of children in each group. "Fasten-ating"!

Laundry Learning Center

To prepare for this center, gather a supply of baby clothes with a variety of snaps, buttons, and zippers. (Ask parents for donations, or check thrift stores and yard sales.) Wash the clothes and then place them in a laundry basket. Place the basket in a center along with a variety of stuffed animals that will fit into the clothes. Invite each child to put the clothing on the animals and then fasten the zippers, buttons, or snaps. To add a little zip to this activity, invite each child to sing "A Snappy Song" (page 187) as she works.

A Snappy Song

What's the best way to refine those self-help skills? Practice, practice, practice! So invite your youngsters to act out this lively tune and get those little fingers snapping, buttoning, and zipping!

(sung to the tune of "Down by the Station")

Chorus:
Snap, button, zipper,
See them on my clothing!
I can button, snap, and zip
All by myself!

See how I can zip up
All the little zippers.
Zip, zip! Zip, zip!
Off I go!

Repeat Chorus

See how I can snap up
All the little snappies.
Snap, snap! Snap, snap!
Off I go!

Repeat Chorus

See how I can button
All the little buttons.
Button, button! Button, button!
Off I go!

Snap to It!

Snap! Snap! Snap! That's the sound you'll hear at this matching center. In advance, gather a supply of old shirts with snaps. (Check thrift stores, or ask parents for donations.) Snap up each shirt; then cut off the snap plackets. Next, cut each placket into different lengths. Unsnap the plackets and place them in a basket at a center. Invite each child to explore the strips and snap together the different pieces. For older students, have each child match the snaps by fabric design and length. Then have her snap the strips together.

Zip-a-dee-doo-dah!

Jeans, jackets, pocketbooks, pencil pouches. They all have zippers! Stock a center with a variety of zippered items such as these. Then invite youngsters to zip and unzip away! Zip-a-dee-doo-dah! Zip-a-dee-ay! My, oh my, what a wonderful way...to practice zipping!

Mary Lester

If You're Happy and You Know It

Get your preschoolers singing about the feeling we all like best—being happy. Then use the familiar song as a springboard into literacy and creativity with the following learning activities.

by Lucia Kemp Henry

If you're happy and you know it, clap your hands.
If you're happy and you know it, clap your hands.
If you're happy and you know it, then your face will surely show it.
If you're happy and you know it, clap your hands.

Sing-Along Booklet

These personalized song booklets are sure to make everyone happy. How will you know it? Everyone will be smiling as they "read" and sing along! Duplicate the booklet backing on page 189 onto white construction paper and the booklet pages on pages 189 and 190 onto copy paper to create a class supply. For each child, cut the pages apart and bind them together as shown. Have each child dictate his own action for the song on page 5 of the booklet; then have him color his pages and the child on the cover to resemble himself. If desired, add wiggle eyes stickers and a small pom-pom nose to the child's cover illustration. Have the children take the booklets home to share with their families.

Your Face Will Surely Show It!

Use youngsters' creativity to make this display titled "We're Happy and We Know It. Our Faces Surely Show It!" To prepare an art area, provide several shallow pans of different colors of skin-toned paint and as many circular sponges as you have different colors of paint. Provide each child with a piece of construction paper personalized with the phrase shown. Have each child use a sponge to print a circle on his paper. Then, when the paint is dry, encourage him to use various art supplies— such as strips of crinkled paper, yarn, wiggle eyes stickers, buttons, and markers—to decorate his circle to resemble his face. Display the pages together on the titled background. Smiling faces in happy places!

Name _____

If You're Happy and You Know It

5

Staple pages here.

1

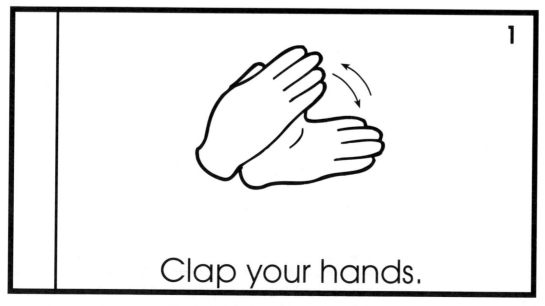

Clap your hands.

Booklet Patterns
Use with "Sing-Along Booklet" on page 188.

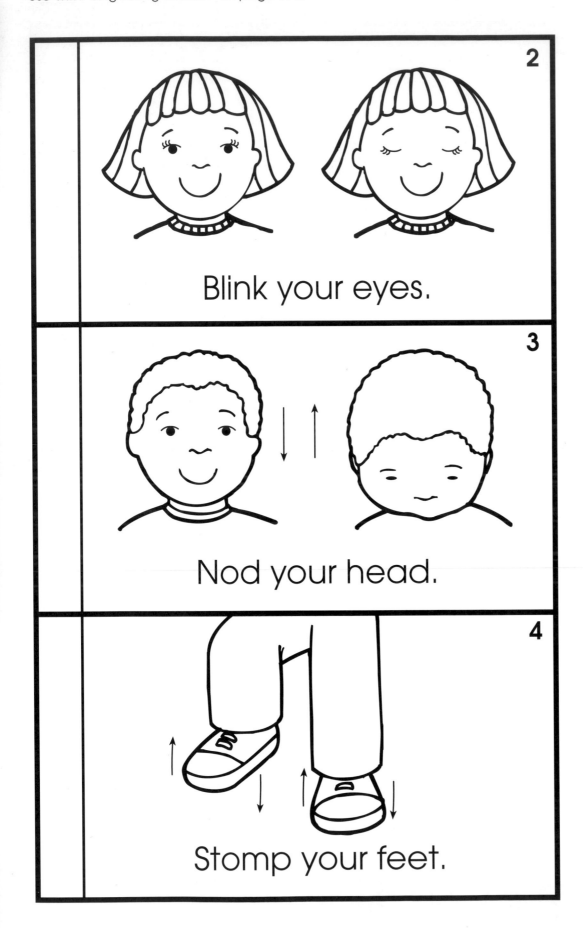

2

Blink your eyes.

3

Nod your head.

4

Stomp your feet.

Classroom by Design

Create a fun and colorful environment for your preschoolers with these simple yet innovative decorating ideas.

ideas by dayle timmons—Special Education-Inclusion, Alimacani Elementary School, Jacksonville, FL

Curtain Time!

Add warmth and color with these easy-to-make curtains. And the best news is you won't have to sew a stitch! Measure the sides and top of a window. Then obtain a piece of colorful cotton fabric long enough to drape along the top and sides of it. Use pinking shears to cut the ends of the fabric to keep it from unraveling. Next, mount a large, self-adhesive hook over each top corner of the window. If the window is very wide, add a hook in the center as well. Hang a plastic bracelet or shower curtain ring on each hook; then drape the fabric through the rings as shown. If desired, fold pleats along the top of the curtain above the window, securing them with staples or hot glue. Once the curtain goes up, take a bow!

Head for the Border

What's so stylish about this fabric-covered bulletin board border? It matches your curtains! Cut a piece of fabric to fit a large piece of lined poster board (available from office supply stores). Iron fusible webbing to the fabric; then iron the fabric to the poster board. Using the lines as a handy guide, cut the poster board into three-inch-wide strips. If desired, laminate the strips to prevent fraying. Make enough border to frame your board. With this idea, your bulletin boards will really have an edge!

They've Been Framed!

Draw attention to your bulletin boards by framing them with fabric. Simply measure the sides and top of each board; then prepare a fabric drape in the same manner used to make the curtains described in "Curtain Time!" Add a few pushpins along the top and sides of the fabric drape to keep the material securely in place.

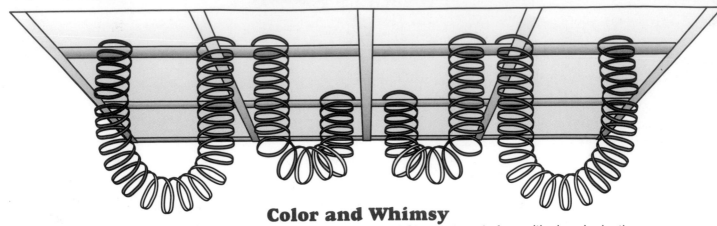

Color and Whimsy

Create rainbows of color on your ceiling with this unique idea! Slip each end of a multicolored, plastic Slinky-type toy into the tiles of your ceiling so that it hangs down in a loop. Hang a number of these around your room for a display that causes everyone who enters to do a double take. What a way to top off your classroom decorations!

Made in the Shade

A colorful beach umbrella can brighten any classroom. Purchase an inexpensive beach umbrella. (Watch for sales toward summer's end.) To anchor the umbrella, half-fill a sand pail with plaster of paris. Prop the umbrella in an upright position in the plaster until it dries. Later, fill the rest of the pail with sand and some shells. Finally, place the umbrella on a table in a learning center. Cool idea, dude!

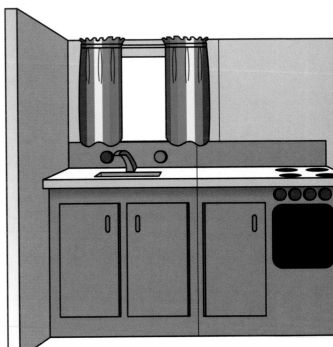

Puppet Window

If you have a three-piece folding puppet theater and not a lot of storage space, this idea is for you! Store the puppet theater in your dramatic play area behind the pretend sink. You will have more storage space and your little ones will have a window they can look out as they wash, wash, wash the dishes!

ABCs and 123s

Wow! This alternative to your traditional alphabet or number line is really eye-catching! Simply use double-sided tape or Sticky-Tac to attach interlocking foam alphabet or number squares to your wall. Or hot-glue the squares to the wall if it is a surface from which the glue can later be removed. If you have an incomplete set of letters or numbers, connect the pieces in random order; then attach them to your bathroom walls as a border.